S0-ARA-126

# Dream journal

Keep Track Books

*Keep Track Books* brings you a variety of
essential notebooks and journals — including
dream journals with the same interior as this one,
but with different cover designs.

Please visit www.lusciousbooks.co.uk to find out more.

CreateSpace, Charleston SC
Design © Keep Track Books

All rights reserved
No part of this publication may be reproduced, stored in a retrieval system, or transmitted in any form or
by any means, electronic, mechanical, photocopying, recording or otherwise, without the prior written
permission of the copyright owner.

Unauthorised reproduction of any part of this publication by any means including photocopying is an
infringement of copyright.

# Dreams are precious gifts

They are windows to your innermost self and through them you can learn more about
your subconscious feelings, increase your self-awareness, access your creativity
and be guided by your inner wisdom.

## How to use this dream journal

Dreams are easily lost if they are not written down. Therefore, it's good to keep
your dream journal by your bed and write down your dream as soon as you wake up.
If you can't remember the whole dream, write down any feelings, thoughts or
images that come to mind. Don't judge what you're writing – just let everything
flow onto the page freely. Once you have done this, give your dream a title
and add the date.

This journal contains prompts to help you analyse and interpret your dreams.
You don't have to fill in all the sections and you don't have to answer the questions
in the order that they are laid out on the page. Start by filling in the sections
that feel the easiest to answer.

You don't have to write down your dream and interpret it all in one go.
If you feel that the answers are not flowing easily, leave the analysis for another time.
Sometimes it takes a while to fully understand what a specific dream is about.

May your dream exploration be filled with
exciting discoveries and profound insights!

Dream title:                                    Date:

## Dream description

..............................................................................................................
..............................................................................................................
..............................................................................................................
..............................................................................................................
..............................................................................................................
..............................................................................................................
..............................................................................................................
..............................................................................................................
..............................................................................................................
..............................................................................................................
..............................................................................................................
..............................................................................................................
..............................................................................................................
..............................................................................................................
..............................................................................................................
..............................................................................................................
..............................................................................................................
..............................................................................................................
..............................................................................................................
..............................................................................................................
..............................................................................................................
..............................................................................................................
..............................................................................................................
..............................................................................................................
..............................................................................................................
..............................................................................................................
..............................................................................................................
..............................................................................................................
..............................................................................................................
..............................................................................................................

Was this dream...    a recurring dream?    a lucid dream?    a nightmare?
☐ Yes  ☐ No    ☐ Yes  ☐ No    ☐ Yes  ☐ No

## What were the key themes or issues in the dream?

..............................................................................................................................

..............................................................................................................................

..............................................................................................................................

## What were your prominent emotions and feelings?

| | | | | |
|---|---|---|---|---|
| ☐ Happiness | ☐ Surprise | ☐ Indifference | ☐ Fear | ☐ Disapproval |
| ☐ Love | ☐ Joy | ☐ Sadness | ☐ Panic | ☐ Rejection |
| ☐ Freedom | ☐ Contentment | ☐ Frustration | ☐ Envy | ☐ Anxiety |
| ☐ Compassion | ☐ Pride | ☐ Betrayal | ☐ Jealousy | ☐ Guilt |
| ☐ Arousal | ☐ Confusion | ☐ Anger | ☐ Shame | ☐ Pain |
| Other? | ☐ | | ☐ | |
| | ☐ | | ☐ | |

## Could this dream relate to a recent situation/event/person/problem in your life?

..............................................................................................................................

..............................................................................................................................

..............................................................................................................................

## What is your interpretation of the dream?

..............................................................................................................................

..............................................................................................................................

..............................................................................................................................

..............................................................................................................................

..............................................................................................................................

..............................................................................................................................

..............................................................................................................................

## In what way(s) does this dream affect you?
### Does it provide clarity into something or suggest a specific course of action?

..............................................................................................................................

..............................................................................................................................

..............................................................................................................................

Dream title: _____  Date:

## Dream description

..................................................................................................................
..................................................................................................................
..................................................................................................................
..................................................................................................................
..................................................................................................................
..................................................................................................................
..................................................................................................................
..................................................................................................................
..................................................................................................................
..................................................................................................................
..................................................................................................................
..................................................................................................................
..................................................................................................................
..................................................................................................................
..................................................................................................................
..................................................................................................................
..................................................................................................................
..................................................................................................................
..................................................................................................................
..................................................................................................................
..................................................................................................................
..................................................................................................................
..................................................................................................................
..................................................................................................................
..................................................................................................................
..................................................................................................................
..................................................................................................................
..................................................................................................................
..................................................................................................................
..................................................................................................................
..................................................................................................................
..................................................................................................................
..................................................................................................................
..................................................................................................................

Was this dream...   a recurring dream?   a lucid dream?   a nightmare?
                    ☐ Yes  ☐ No        ☐ Yes  ☐ No     ☐ Yes  ☐ No

## What were the key themes or issues in the dream?

........................................................................................................

........................................................................................................

........................................................................................................

## What were your prominent emotions and feelings?

| | | | | |
|---|---|---|---|---|
| ☐ Happiness | ☐ Surprise | ☐ Indifference | ☐ Fear | ☐ Disapproval |
| ☐ Love | ☐ Joy | ☐ Sadness | ☐ Panic | ☐ Rejection |
| ☐ Freedom | ☐ Contentment | ☐ Frustration | ☐ Envy | ☐ Anxiety |
| ☐ Compassion | ☐ Pride | ☐ Betrayal | ☐ Jealousy | ☐ Guilt |
| ☐ Arousal | ☐ Confusion | ☐ Anger | ☐ Shame | ☐ Pain |
| Other? | ☐ | | ☐ | |
| | ☐ | | ☐ | |

## Could this dream relate to a recent situation/event/person/problem in your life?

........................................................................................................

........................................................................................................

........................................................................................................

## What is your interpretation of the dream?

........................................................................................................

........................................................................................................

........................................................................................................

........................................................................................................

........................................................................................................

........................................................................................................

## In what way(s) does this dream affect you?
## Does it provide clarity into something or suggest a specific course of action?

........................................................................................................

........................................................................................................

........................................................................................................

Dream title: _____ Date: _____

## Dream description

..........................................................................
..........................................................................
..........................................................................
..........................................................................
..........................................................................
..........................................................................
..........................................................................
..........................................................................
..........................................................................
..........................................................................
..........................................................................
..........................................................................
..........................................................................
..........................................................................
..........................................................................
..........................................................................
..........................................................................
..........................................................................
..........................................................................
..........................................................................
..........................................................................
..........................................................................
..........................................................................
..........................................................................
..........................................................................
..........................................................................
..........................................................................
..........................................................................
..........................................................................
..........................................................................

Was this dream...  a recurring dream?   a lucid dream?   a nightmare?
☐ Yes ☐ No          ☐ Yes ☐ No      ☐ Yes ☐ No

## What were the key themes or issues in the dream?

.......................................................................................................................................
.......................................................................................................................................
.......................................................................................................................................

## What were your prominent emotions and feelings?

| | | | | |
|---|---|---|---|---|
| ☐ Happiness | ☐ Surprise | ☐ Indifference | ☐ Fear | ☐ Disapproval |
| ☐ Love | ☐ Joy | ☐ Sadness | ☐ Panic | ☐ Rejection |
| ☐ Freedom | ☐ Contentment | ☐ Frustration | ☐ Envy | ☐ Anxiety |
| ☐ Compassion | ☐ Pride | ☐ Betrayal | ☐ Jealousy | ☐ Guilt |
| ☐ Arousal | ☐ Confusion | ☐ Anger | ☐ Shame | ☐ Pain |

Other?
☐ .................................................. ☐ ..................................................
☐ .................................................. ☐ ..................................................

## Could this dream relate to a recent situation/event/person/problem in your life?

.......................................................................................................................................
.......................................................................................................................................
.......................................................................................................................................

## What is your interpretation of the dream?

.......................................................................................................................................
.......................................................................................................................................
.......................................................................................................................................
.......................................................................................................................................
.......................................................................................................................................
.......................................................................................................................................
.......................................................................................................................................

## In what way(s) does this dream affect you?
## Does it provide clarity into something or suggest a specific course of action?

.......................................................................................................................................
.......................................................................................................................................
.......................................................................................................................................

Dream title:                                                    Date:

## Dream description

........................................................................................
........................................................................................
........................................................................................
........................................................................................
........................................................................................
........................................................................................
........................................................................................
........................................................................................
........................................................................................
........................................................................................
........................................................................................
........................................................................................
........................................................................................
........................................................................................
........................................................................................
........................................................................................
........................................................................................
........................................................................................
........................................................................................
........................................................................................
........................................................................................
........................................................................................
........................................................................................
........................................................................................
........................................................................................
........................................................................................
........................................................................................
........................................................................................
........................................................................................
........................................................................................
........................................................................................
........................................................................................
........................................................................................

Was this dream...

| | a recurring dream? | a lucid dream? | a nightmare? |
|---|---|---|---|
| | ☐ Yes  ☐ No | ☐ Yes  ☐ No | ☐ Yes  ☐ No |

## What were the key themes or issues in the dream?

......................................................................................................

......................................................................................................

......................................................................................................

## What were your prominent emotions and feelings?

| | | | | |
|---|---|---|---|---|
| ☐ Happiness | ☐ Surprise | ☐ Indifference | ☐ Fear | ☐ Disapproval |
| ☐ Love | ☐ Joy | ☐ Sadness | ☐ Panic | ☐ Rejection |
| ☐ Freedom | ☐ Contentment | ☐ Frustration | ☐ Envy | ☐ Anxiety |
| ☐ Compassion | ☐ Pride | ☐ Betrayal | ☐ Jealousy | ☐ Guilt |
| ☐ Arousal | ☐ Confusion | ☐ Anger | ☐ Shame | ☐ Pain |
| Other? | ☐ ................ | | ☐ ................ | |
| | ☐ ................ | | ☐ ................ | |

## Could this dream relate to a recent situation/event/person/problem in your life?

......................................................................................................

......................................................................................................

......................................................................................................

## What is your interpretation of the dream?

......................................................................................................

......................................................................................................

......................................................................................................

......................................................................................................

......................................................................................................

......................................................................................................

## In what way(s) does this dream affect you?
## Does it provide clarity into something or suggest a specific course of action?

......................................................................................................

......................................................................................................

......................................................................................................

Dream title:                                                      Date:

## Dream description

...........................................................................................................................
...........................................................................................................................
...........................................................................................................................
...........................................................................................................................
...........................................................................................................................
...........................................................................................................................
...........................................................................................................................
...........................................................................................................................
...........................................................................................................................
...........................................................................................................................
...........................................................................................................................
...........................................................................................................................
...........................................................................................................................
...........................................................................................................................
...........................................................................................................................
...........................................................................................................................
...........................................................................................................................
...........................................................................................................................
...........................................................................................................................
...........................................................................................................................
...........................................................................................................................
...........................................................................................................................
...........................................................................................................................
...........................................................................................................................
...........................................................................................................................
...........................................................................................................................
...........................................................................................................................
...........................................................................................................................
...........................................................................................................................
...........................................................................................................................
...........................................................................................................................

Was this dream...    a recurring dream?    a lucid dream?    a nightmare?
　　　　　　　　　　　☐ Yes  ☐ No    ☐ Yes  ☐ No    ☐ Yes  ☐ No

## What were the key themes or issues in the dream?

.......................................................................................................................

.......................................................................................................................

.......................................................................................................................

## What were your prominent emotions and feelings?

| | | | | |
|---|---|---|---|---|
| ☐ Happiness | ☐ Surprise | ☐ Indifference | ☐ Fear | ☐ Disapproval |
| ☐ Love | ☐ Joy | ☐ Sadness | ☐ Panic | ☐ Rejection |
| ☐ Freedom | ☐ Contentment | ☐ Frustration | ☐ Envy | ☐ Anxiety |
| ☐ Compassion | ☐ Pride | ☐ Betrayal | ☐ Jealousy | ☐ Guilt |
| ☐ Arousal | ☐ Confusion | ☐ Anger | ☐ Shame | ☐ Pain |

Other?　☐ ..................................　☐ ..................................

　　　　☐ ..................................　☐ ..................................

## Could this dream relate to a recent situation/event/person/problem in your life?

.......................................................................................................................

.......................................................................................................................

.......................................................................................................................

## What is your interpretation of the dream?

.......................................................................................................................

.......................................................................................................................

.......................................................................................................................

.......................................................................................................................

.......................................................................................................................

.......................................................................................................................

.......................................................................................................................

## In what way(s) does this dream affect you?
## Does it provide clarity into something or suggest a specific course of action?

.......................................................................................................................

.......................................................................................................................

.......................................................................................................................

Dream title:                                              Date:

## Dream description

...................................................................................................................
...................................................................................................................
...................................................................................................................
...................................................................................................................
...................................................................................................................
...................................................................................................................
...................................................................................................................
...................................................................................................................
...................................................................................................................
...................................................................................................................
...................................................................................................................
...................................................................................................................
...................................................................................................................
...................................................................................................................
...................................................................................................................
...................................................................................................................
...................................................................................................................
...................................................................................................................
...................................................................................................................
...................................................................................................................
...................................................................................................................
...................................................................................................................
...................................................................................................................
...................................................................................................................
...................................................................................................................
...................................................................................................................
...................................................................................................................
...................................................................................................................
...................................................................................................................
...................................................................................................................

Was this dream...   a recurring dream?     a lucid dream?       a nightmare?
                    ☐ Yes  ☐ No           ☐ Yes  ☐ No          ☐ Yes  ☐ No

## What were the key themes or issues in the dream?

..........................................................................................................

..........................................................................................................

..........................................................................................................

## What were your prominent emotions and feelings?

| | | | | |
|---|---|---|---|---|
| ☐ Happiness | ☐ Surprise | ☐ Indifference | ☐ Fear | ☐ Disapproval |
| ☐ Love | ☐ Joy | ☐ Sadness | ☐ Panic | ☐ Rejection |
| ☐ Freedom | ☐ Contentment | ☐ Frustration | ☐ Envy | ☐ Anxiety |
| ☐ Compassion | ☐ Pride | ☐ Betrayal | ☐ Jealousy | ☐ Guilt |
| ☐ Arousal | ☐ Confusion | ☐ Anger | ☐ Shame | ☐ Pain |

Other?   ☐ ...............................   ☐ ...............................

         ☐ ...............................   ☐ ...............................

## Could this dream relate to a recent situation/event/person/problem in your life?

..........................................................................................................

..........................................................................................................

..........................................................................................................

## What is your interpretation of the dream?

..........................................................................................................

..........................................................................................................

..........................................................................................................

..........................................................................................................

..........................................................................................................

..........................................................................................................

## In what way(s) does this dream affect you?
## Does it provide clarity into something or suggest a specific course of action?

..........................................................................................................

..........................................................................................................

..........................................................................................................

Dream title: _____     Date: _____

## Dream description

..........................................................................................................
..........................................................................................................
..........................................................................................................
..........................................................................................................
..........................................................................................................
..........................................................................................................
..........................................................................................................
..........................................................................................................
..........................................................................................................
..........................................................................................................
..........................................................................................................
..........................................................................................................
..........................................................................................................
..........................................................................................................
..........................................................................................................
..........................................................................................................
..........................................................................................................
..........................................................................................................
..........................................................................................................
..........................................................................................................
..........................................................................................................
..........................................................................................................
..........................................................................................................
..........................................................................................................
..........................................................................................................
..........................................................................................................
..........................................................................................................
..........................................................................................................
..........................................................................................................
..........................................................................................................

Was this dream...      a recurring dream?      a lucid dream?      a nightmare?
☐ Yes  ☐ No            ☐ Yes  ☐ No            ☐ Yes  ☐ No

## What were the key themes or issues in the dream?

..................................................................................................

..................................................................................................

..................................................................................................

## What were your prominent emotions and feelings?

| | | | | |
|---|---|---|---|---|
| ☐ Happiness | ☐ Surprise | ☐ Indifference | ☐ Fear | ☐ Disapproval |
| ☐ Love | ☐ Joy | ☐ Sadness | ☐ Panic | ☐ Rejection |
| ☐ Freedom | ☐ Contentment | ☐ Frustration | ☐ Envy | ☐ Anxiety |
| ☐ Compassion | ☐ Pride | ☐ Betrayal | ☐ Jealousy | ☐ Guilt |
| ☐ Arousal | ☐ Confusion | ☐ Anger | ☐ Shame | ☐ Pain |

Other?    ☐ ...........................    ☐ ...........................

☐ ...........................    ☐ ...........................

## Could this dream relate to a recent situation/event/person/problem in your life?

..................................................................................................

..................................................................................................

..................................................................................................

## What is your interpretation of the dream?

..................................................................................................

..................................................................................................

..................................................................................................

..................................................................................................

..................................................................................................

..................................................................................................

## In what way(s) does this dream affect you?
## Does it provide clarity into something or suggest a specific course of action?

..................................................................................................

..................................................................................................

..................................................................................................

Dream title:                                                    Date:

## Dream description

.............................................................................................................
.............................................................................................................
.............................................................................................................
.............................................................................................................
.............................................................................................................
.............................................................................................................
.............................................................................................................
.............................................................................................................
.............................................................................................................
.............................................................................................................
.............................................................................................................
.............................................................................................................
.............................................................................................................
.............................................................................................................
.............................................................................................................
.............................................................................................................
.............................................................................................................
.............................................................................................................
.............................................................................................................
.............................................................................................................
.............................................................................................................
.............................................................................................................
.............................................................................................................
.............................................................................................................
.............................................................................................................
.............................................................................................................
.............................................................................................................
.............................................................................................................
.............................................................................................................
.............................................................................................................
.............................................................................................................
.............................................................................................................

| Was this dream... | a recurring dream? | a lucid dream? | a nightmare? |
|---|---|---|---|
| | ☐ Yes ☐ No | ☐ Yes ☐ No | ☐ Yes ☐ No |

## What were the key themes or issues in the dream?

................................................................................................................

................................................................................................................

................................................................................................................

## What were your prominent emotions and feelings?

| | | | | |
|---|---|---|---|---|
| ☐ Happiness | ☐ Surprise | ☐ Indifference | ☐ Fear | ☐ Disapproval |
| ☐ Love | ☐ Joy | ☐ Sadness | ☐ Panic | ☐ Rejection |
| ☐ Freedom | ☐ Contentment | ☐ Frustration | ☐ Envy | ☐ Anxiety |
| ☐ Compassion | ☐ Pride | ☐ Betrayal | ☐ Jealousy | ☐ Guilt |
| ☐ Arousal | ☐ Confusion | ☐ Anger | ☐ Shame | ☐ Pain |
| Other? | ☐ ................... | | ☐ ................... | |
| | ☐ ................... | | ☐ ................... | |

## Could this dream relate to a recent situation/event/person/problem in your life?

................................................................................................................

................................................................................................................

................................................................................................................

## What is your interpretation of the dream?

................................................................................................................

................................................................................................................

................................................................................................................

................................................................................................................

................................................................................................................

................................................................................................................

## In what way(s) does this dream affect you?
## Does it provide clarity into something or suggest a specific course of action?

................................................................................................................

................................................................................................................

................................................................................................................

Dream title: _____  Date: _____

## Dream description

..........................................................................................................
..........................................................................................................
..........................................................................................................
..........................................................................................................
..........................................................................................................
..........................................................................................................
..........................................................................................................
..........................................................................................................
..........................................................................................................
..........................................................................................................
..........................................................................................................
..........................................................................................................
..........................................................................................................
..........................................................................................................
..........................................................................................................
..........................................................................................................
..........................................................................................................
..........................................................................................................
..........................................................................................................
..........................................................................................................
..........................................................................................................
..........................................................................................................
..........................................................................................................
..........................................................................................................
..........................................................................................................
..........................................................................................................
..........................................................................................................
..........................................................................................................
..........................................................................................................
..........................................................................................................
..........................................................................................................

Was this dream...      a recurring dream?      a lucid dream?      a nightmare?
                       ☐ Yes   ☐ No           ☐ Yes   ☐ No         ☐ Yes   ☐ No

## What were the key themes or issues in the dream?

.......................................................................................
.......................................................................................
.......................................................................................

## What were your prominent emotions and feelings?

☐ Happiness      ☐ Surprise       ☐ Indifference     ☐ Fear        ☐ Disapproval
☐ Love           ☐ Joy            ☐ Sadness          ☐ Panic       ☐ Rejection
☐ Freedom        ☐ Contentment    ☐ Frustration      ☐ Envy        ☐ Anxiety
☐ Compassion     ☐ Pride          ☐ Betrayal         ☐ Jealousy    ☐ Guilt
☐ Arousal        ☐ Confusion      ☐ Anger            ☐ Shame       ☐ Pain
Other?           ☐                                   ☐
                 ....................................  .......................................
                 ☐                                   ☐
                 ....................................  .......................................

## Could this dream relate to a recent situation/event/person/problem in your life?

.......................................................................................
.......................................................................................
.......................................................................................

## What is your interpretation of the dream?

.......................................................................................
.......................................................................................
.......................................................................................
.......................................................................................
.......................................................................................
.......................................................................................
.......................................................................................

## In what way(s) does this dream affect you?
## Does it provide clarity into something or suggest a specific course of action?

.......................................................................................
.......................................................................................
.......................................................................................

Dream title: _____ Date: _____

## Dream description

.......................................................................................................
.......................................................................................................
.......................................................................................................
.......................................................................................................
.......................................................................................................
.......................................................................................................
.......................................................................................................
.......................................................................................................
.......................................................................................................
.......................................................................................................
.......................................................................................................
.......................................................................................................
.......................................................................................................
.......................................................................................................
.......................................................................................................
.......................................................................................................
.......................................................................................................
.......................................................................................................
.......................................................................................................
.......................................................................................................
.......................................................................................................
.......................................................................................................
.......................................................................................................
.......................................................................................................
.......................................................................................................
.......................................................................................................
.......................................................................................................
.......................................................................................................
.......................................................................................................
.......................................................................................................
.......................................................................................................
.......................................................................................................

Was this dream...      a recurring dream?      a lucid dream?      a nightmare?

☐ Yes  ☐ No      ☐ Yes  ☐ No      ☐ Yes  ☐ No

## What were the key themes or issues in the dream?

..........................................................................................................
..........................................................................................................
..........................................................................................................

## What were your prominent emotions and feelings?

| | | | | |
|---|---|---|---|---|
| ☐ Happiness | ☐ Surprise | ☐ Indifference | ☐ Fear | ☐ Disapproval |
| ☐ Love | ☐ Joy | ☐ Sadness | ☐ Panic | ☐ Rejection |
| ☐ Freedom | ☐ Contentment | ☐ Frustration | ☐ Envy | ☐ Anxiety |
| ☐ Compassion | ☐ Pride | ☐ Betrayal | ☐ Jealousy | ☐ Guilt |
| ☐ Arousal | ☐ Confusion | ☐ Anger | ☐ Shame | ☐ Pain |

Other?    ☐ ................................    ☐ ................................

       ☐ ................................    ☐ ................................

## Could this dream relate to a recent situation/event/person/problem in your life?

..........................................................................................................
..........................................................................................................
..........................................................................................................

## What is your interpretation of the dream?

..........................................................................................................
..........................................................................................................
..........................................................................................................
..........................................................................................................
..........................................................................................................
..........................................................................................................

## In what way(s) does this dream affect you?
## Does it provide clarity into something or suggest a specific course of action?

..........................................................................................................
..........................................................................................................
..........................................................................................................

Dream title: _____ Date: _____

## Dream description

........................................................................................................
........................................................................................................
........................................................................................................
........................................................................................................
........................................................................................................
........................................................................................................
........................................................................................................
........................................................................................................
........................................................................................................
........................................................................................................
........................................................................................................
........................................................................................................
........................................................................................................
........................................................................................................
........................................................................................................
........................................................................................................
........................................................................................................
........................................................................................................
........................................................................................................
........................................................................................................
........................................................................................................
........................................................................................................
........................................................................................................
........................................................................................................
........................................................................................................
........................................................................................................
........................................................................................................
........................................................................................................
........................................................................................................
........................................................................................................
........................................................................................................
........................................................................................................

Was this dream...  a recurring dream?  a lucid dream?  a nightmare?
                   ☐ Yes  ☐ No      ☐ Yes  ☐ No    ☐ Yes  ☐ No

## What were the key themes or issues in the dream?

...................................................................................................

...................................................................................................

...................................................................................................

## What were your prominent emotions and feelings?

| | | | | |
|---|---|---|---|---|
| ☐ Happiness | ☐ Surprise | ☐ Indifference | ☐ Fear | ☐ Disapproval |
| ☐ Love | ☐ Joy | ☐ Sadness | ☐ Panic | ☐ Rejection |
| ☐ Freedom | ☐ Contentment | ☐ Frustration | ☐ Envy | ☐ Anxiety |
| ☐ Compassion | ☐ Pride | ☐ Betrayal | ☐ Jealousy | ☐ Guilt |
| ☐ Arousal | ☐ Confusion | ☐ Anger | ☐ Shame | ☐ Pain |

Other?
☐ ...........................................  ☐ ...........................................
☐ ...........................................  ☐ ...........................................

## Could this dream relate to a recent situation/event/person/problem in your life?

...................................................................................................

...................................................................................................

...................................................................................................

## What is your interpretation of the dream?

...................................................................................................

...................................................................................................

...................................................................................................

...................................................................................................

...................................................................................................

...................................................................................................

## In what way(s) does this dream affect you?
## Does it provide clarity into something or suggest a specific course of action?

...................................................................................................

...................................................................................................

...................................................................................................

Dream title:                                          Date:

## Dream description

..............................................................................................................................
..............................................................................................................................
..............................................................................................................................
..............................................................................................................................
..............................................................................................................................
..............................................................................................................................
..............................................................................................................................
..............................................................................................................................
..............................................................................................................................
..............................................................................................................................
..............................................................................................................................
..............................................................................................................................
..............................................................................................................................
..............................................................................................................................
..............................................................................................................................
..............................................................................................................................
..............................................................................................................................
..............................................................................................................................
..............................................................................................................................
..............................................................................................................................
..............................................................................................................................
..............................................................................................................................
..............................................................................................................................
..............................................................................................................................
..............................................................................................................................
..............................................................................................................................
..............................................................................................................................
..............................................................................................................................
..............................................................................................................................
..............................................................................................................................
..............................................................................................................................
..............................................................................................................................

Was this dream...    a recurring dream?    a lucid dream?    a nightmare?
☐ Yes  ☐ No    ☐ Yes  ☐ No    ☐ Yes  ☐ No

## What were the key themes or issues in the dream?

...............................................................................................................................
...............................................................................................................................
...............................................................................................................................

## What were your prominent emotions and feelings?

| | | | | |
|---|---|---|---|---|
| ☐ Happiness | ☐ Surprise | ☐ Indifference | ☐ Fear | ☐ Disapproval |
| ☐ Love | ☐ Joy | ☐ Sadness | ☐ Panic | ☐ Rejection |
| ☐ Freedom | ☐ Contentment | ☐ Frustration | ☐ Envy | ☐ Anxiety |
| ☐ Compassion | ☐ Pride | ☐ Betrayal | ☐ Jealousy | ☐ Guilt |
| ☐ Arousal | ☐ Confusion | ☐ Anger | ☐ Shame | ☐ Pain |

Other?    ☐ .................................    ☐ .................................
        ☐ .................................    ☐ .................................

## Could this dream relate to a recent situation/event/person/problem in your life?

...............................................................................................................................
...............................................................................................................................
...............................................................................................................................

## What is your interpretation of the dream?

...............................................................................................................................
...............................................................................................................................
...............................................................................................................................
...............................................................................................................................
...............................................................................................................................
...............................................................................................................................

## In what way(s) does this dream affect you?
## Does it provide clarity into something or suggest a specific course of action?

...............................................................................................................................
...............................................................................................................................
...............................................................................................................................

Dream title:                                                    Date:

## Dream description

.......................................................................................................
.......................................................................................................
.......................................................................................................
.......................................................................................................
.......................................................................................................
.......................................................................................................
.......................................................................................................
.......................................................................................................
.......................................................................................................
.......................................................................................................
.......................................................................................................
.......................................................................................................
.......................................................................................................
.......................................................................................................
.......................................................................................................
.......................................................................................................
.......................................................................................................
.......................................................................................................
.......................................................................................................
.......................................................................................................
.......................................................................................................
.......................................................................................................
.......................................................................................................
.......................................................................................................
.......................................................................................................
.......................................................................................................
.......................................................................................................
.......................................................................................................
.......................................................................................................
.......................................................................................................
.......................................................................................................
.......................................................................................................

Was this dream...

| | a recurring dream? | a lucid dream? | a nightmare? |
|---|---|---|---|
| | ☐ Yes ☐ No | ☐ Yes ☐ No | ☐ Yes ☐ No |

## What were the key themes or issues in the dream?

..............................................................................................................................

..............................................................................................................................

..............................................................................................................................

## What were your prominent emotions and feelings?

| | | | | |
|---|---|---|---|---|
| ☐ Happiness | ☐ Surprise | ☐ Indifference | ☐ Fear | ☐ Disapproval |
| ☐ Love | ☐ Joy | ☐ Sadness | ☐ Panic | ☐ Rejection |
| ☐ Freedom | ☐ Contentment | ☐ Frustration | ☐ Envy | ☐ Anxiety |
| ☐ Compassion | ☐ Pride | ☐ Betrayal | ☐ Jealousy | ☐ Guilt |
| ☐ Arousal | ☐ Confusion | ☐ Anger | ☐ Shame | ☐ Pain |
| Other? | ☐ ............................ | | ☐ ............................ | |
| | ☐ ............................ | | ☐ ............................ | |

## Could this dream relate to a recent situation/event/person/problem in your life?

..............................................................................................................................

..............................................................................................................................

..............................................................................................................................

## What is your interpretation of the dream?

..............................................................................................................................

..............................................................................................................................

..............................................................................................................................

..............................................................................................................................

..............................................................................................................................

..............................................................................................................................

## In what way(s) does this dream affect you?
## Does it provide clarity into something or suggest a specific course of action?

..............................................................................................................................

..............................................................................................................................

..............................................................................................................................

Dream title:                                          Date:

## Dream description

..............................................................................................
..............................................................................................
..............................................................................................
..............................................................................................
..............................................................................................
..............................................................................................
..............................................................................................
..............................................................................................
..............................................................................................
..............................................................................................
..............................................................................................
..............................................................................................
..............................................................................................
..............................................................................................
..............................................................................................
..............................................................................................
..............................................................................................
..............................................................................................
..............................................................................................
..............................................................................................
..............................................................................................
..............................................................................................
..............................................................................................
..............................................................................................
..............................................................................................
..............................................................................................
..............................................................................................
..............................................................................................
..............................................................................................
..............................................................................................
..............................................................................................
..............................................................................................

| Was this dream... | a recurring dream? | a lucid dream? | a nightmare? |
|---|---|---|---|
| | ☐ Yes ☐ No | ☐ Yes ☐ No | ☐ Yes ☐ No |

## What were the key themes or issues in the dream?

.......................................................................................................................

.......................................................................................................................

.......................................................................................................................

## What were your prominent emotions and feelings?

| | | | | |
|---|---|---|---|---|
| ☐ Happiness | ☐ Surprise | ☐ Indifference | ☐ Fear | ☐ Disapproval |
| ☐ Love | ☐ Joy | ☐ Sadness | ☐ Panic | ☐ Rejection |
| ☐ Freedom | ☐ Contentment | ☐ Frustration | ☐ Envy | ☐ Anxiety |
| ☐ Compassion | ☐ Pride | ☐ Betrayal | ☐ Jealousy | ☐ Guilt |
| ☐ Arousal | ☐ Confusion | ☐ Anger | ☐ Shame | ☐ Pain |
| Other? | ☐ ................... | | ☐ ................... | |
| | ☐ ................... | | ☐ ................... | |

## Could this dream relate to a recent situation/event/person/problem in your life?

.......................................................................................................................

.......................................................................................................................

.......................................................................................................................

## What is your interpretation of the dream?

.......................................................................................................................

.......................................................................................................................

.......................................................................................................................

.......................................................................................................................

.......................................................................................................................

.......................................................................................................................

.......................................................................................................................

## In what way(s) does this dream affect you?
## Does it provide clarity into something or suggest a specific course of action?

.......................................................................................................................

.......................................................................................................................

.......................................................................................................................

Dream title: _____ Date: _____

## Dream description

..............................................................................................
..............................................................................................
..............................................................................................
..............................................................................................
..............................................................................................
..............................................................................................
..............................................................................................
..............................................................................................
..............................................................................................
..............................................................................................
..............................................................................................
..............................................................................................
..............................................................................................
..............................................................................................
..............................................................................................
..............................................................................................
..............................................................................................
..............................................................................................
..............................................................................................
..............................................................................................
..............................................................................................
..............................................................................................
..............................................................................................
..............................................................................................
..............................................................................................
..............................................................................................
..............................................................................................
..............................................................................................
..............................................................................................
..............................................................................................
..............................................................................................

Was this dream...   a recurring dream?      a lucid dream?      a nightmare?
                    ☐ Yes  ☐ No            ☐ Yes  ☐ No        ☐ Yes  ☐ No

## What were the key themes or issues in the dream?

.............................................................................................

.............................................................................................

.............................................................................................

## What were your prominent emotions and feelings?

| | | | | |
|---|---|---|---|---|
| ☐ Happiness | ☐ Surprise | ☐ Indifference | ☐ Fear | ☐ Disapproval |
| ☐ Love | ☐ Joy | ☐ Sadness | ☐ Panic | ☐ Rejection |
| ☐ Freedom | ☐ Contentment | ☐ Frustration | ☐ Envy | ☐ Anxiety |
| ☐ Compassion | ☐ Pride | ☐ Betrayal | ☐ Jealousy | ☐ Guilt |
| ☐ Arousal | ☐ Confusion | ☐ Anger | ☐ Shame | ☐ Pain |

Other?  ☐ ....................................  ☐ ....................................

        ☐ ....................................  ☐ ....................................

## Could this dream relate to a recent situation/event/person/problem in your life?

.............................................................................................

.............................................................................................

.............................................................................................

## What is your interpretation of the dream?

.............................................................................................

.............................................................................................

.............................................................................................

.............................................................................................

.............................................................................................

.............................................................................................

.............................................................................................

## In what way(s) does this dream affect you?
## Does it provide clarity into something or suggest a specific course of action?

.............................................................................................

.............................................................................................

.............................................................................................

Dream title:                                                      Date:

## Dream description

..................................................................................................................................
..................................................................................................................................
..................................................................................................................................
..................................................................................................................................
..................................................................................................................................
..................................................................................................................................
..................................................................................................................................
..................................................................................................................................
..................................................................................................................................
..................................................................................................................................
..................................................................................................................................
..................................................................................................................................
..................................................................................................................................
..................................................................................................................................
..................................................................................................................................
..................................................................................................................................
..................................................................................................................................
..................................................................................................................................
..................................................................................................................................
..................................................................................................................................
..................................................................................................................................
..................................................................................................................................
..................................................................................................................................
..................................................................................................................................
..................................................................................................................................
..................................................................................................................................
..................................................................................................................................
..................................................................................................................................
..................................................................................................................................
..................................................................................................................................
..................................................................................................................................
..................................................................................................................................
..................................................................................................................................

Was this dream...    a recurring dream?    a lucid dream?    a nightmare?
☐ Yes  ☐ No    ☐ Yes  ☐ No    ☐ Yes  ☐ No

## What were the key themes or issues in the dream?

..................................................................................................................................
..................................................................................................................................
..................................................................................................................................

## What were your prominent emotions and feelings?

| | | | | |
|---|---|---|---|---|
| ☐ Happiness | ☐ Surprise | ☐ Indifference | ☐ Fear | ☐ Disapproval |
| ☐ Love | ☐ Joy | ☐ Sadness | ☐ Panic | ☐ Rejection |
| ☐ Freedom | ☐ Contentment | ☐ Frustration | ☐ Envy | ☐ Anxiety |
| ☐ Compassion | ☐ Pride | ☐ Betrayal | ☐ Jealousy | ☐ Guilt |
| ☐ Arousal | ☐ Confusion | ☐ Anger | ☐ Shame | ☐ Pain |

Other?
☐ ..............................................    ☐ ..............................................
☐ ..............................................    ☐ ..............................................

## Could this dream relate to a recent situation/event/person/problem in your life?

..................................................................................................................................
..................................................................................................................................
..................................................................................................................................

## What is your interpretation of the dream?

..................................................................................................................................
..................................................................................................................................
..................................................................................................................................
..................................................................................................................................
..................................................................................................................................
..................................................................................................................................
..................................................................................................................................

## In what way(s) does this dream affect you?
## Does it provide clarity into something or suggest a specific course of action?

..................................................................................................................................
..................................................................................................................................
..................................................................................................................................

Dream title:                                    Date:

## Dream description

...........................................................................................................................

...........................................................................................................................

...........................................................................................................................

...........................................................................................................................

...........................................................................................................................

...........................................................................................................................

...........................................................................................................................

...........................................................................................................................

...........................................................................................................................

...........................................................................................................................

...........................................................................................................................

...........................................................................................................................

...........................................................................................................................

...........................................................................................................................

...........................................................................................................................

...........................................................................................................................

...........................................................................................................................

...........................................................................................................................

...........................................................................................................................

...........................................................................................................................

...........................................................................................................................

...........................................................................................................................

...........................................................................................................................

...........................................................................................................................

...........................................................................................................................

...........................................................................................................................

...........................................................................................................................

...........................................................................................................................

...........................................................................................................................

Was this dream...   a recurring dream?     a lucid dream?      a nightmare?
                    ☐ Yes  ☐ No          ☐ Yes  ☐ No         ☐ Yes  ☐ No

## What were the key themes or issues in the dream?

.................................................................................................
.................................................................................................
.................................................................................................

## What were your prominent emotions and feelings?

| ☐ Happiness | ☐ Surprise | ☐ Indifference | ☐ Fear | ☐ Disapproval |
| ☐ Love | ☐ Joy | ☐ Sadness | ☐ Panic | ☐ Rejection |
| ☐ Freedom | ☐ Contentment | ☐ Frustration | ☐ Envy | ☐ Anxiety |
| ☐ Compassion | ☐ Pride | ☐ Betrayal | ☐ Jealousy | ☐ Guilt |
| ☐ Arousal | ☐ Confusion | ☐ Anger | ☐ Shame | ☐ Pain |
| Other? | ☐ ................ | | ☐ ................ | |
| | ☐ ................ | | ☐ ................ | |

## Could this dream relate to a recent situation/event/person/problem in your life?

.................................................................................................
.................................................................................................
.................................................................................................

## What is your interpretation of the dream?

.................................................................................................
.................................................................................................
.................................................................................................
.................................................................................................
.................................................................................................
.................................................................................................
.................................................................................................

## In what way(s) does this dream affect you?
## Does it provide clarity into something or suggest a specific course of action?

.................................................................................................
.................................................................................................
.................................................................................................

Dream title: _____     Date: _____

## Dream description

································································································
································································································
································································································
································································································
································································································
································································································
································································································
································································································
································································································
································································································
································································································
································································································
································································································
································································································
································································································
································································································
································································································
································································································
································································································
································································································
································································································
································································································
································································································
································································································
································································································
································································································
································································································
································································································
································································································
································································································
································································································
································································································
································································································
································································································

Was this dream...
        a recurring dream?     a lucid dream?     a nightmare?
        ☐ Yes ☐ No     ☐ Yes ☐ No     ☐ Yes ☐ No

## What were the key themes or issues in the dream?

......................................................................................................

......................................................................................................

......................................................................................................

## What were your prominent emotions and feelings?

| | | | | |
|---|---|---|---|---|
| ☐ Happiness | ☐ Surprise | ☐ Indifference | ☐ Fear | ☐ Disapproval |
| ☐ Love | ☐ Joy | ☐ Sadness | ☐ Panic | ☐ Rejection |
| ☐ Freedom | ☐ Contentment | ☐ Frustration | ☐ Envy | ☐ Anxiety |
| ☐ Compassion | ☐ Pride | ☐ Betrayal | ☐ Jealousy | ☐ Guilt |
| ☐ Arousal | ☐ Confusion | ☐ Anger | ☐ Shame | ☐ Pain |
| Other? | ☐ .................... | | ☐ .................... | |
| | ☐ .................... | | ☐ .................... | |

## Could this dream relate to a recent situation/event/person/problem in your life?

......................................................................................................

......................................................................................................

......................................................................................................

## What is your interpretation of the dream?

......................................................................................................

......................................................................................................

......................................................................................................

......................................................................................................

......................................................................................................

......................................................................................................

## In what way(s) does this dream affect you?
## Does it provide clarity into something or suggest a specific course of action?

......................................................................................................

......................................................................................................

......................................................................................................

Dream title: _____  Date: _____

## Dream description

.......................................................................................................
.......................................................................................................
.......................................................................................................
.......................................................................................................
.......................................................................................................
.......................................................................................................
.......................................................................................................
.......................................................................................................
.......................................................................................................
.......................................................................................................
.......................................................................................................
.......................................................................................................
.......................................................................................................
.......................................................................................................
.......................................................................................................
.......................................................................................................
.......................................................................................................
.......................................................................................................
.......................................................................................................
.......................................................................................................
.......................................................................................................
.......................................................................................................
.......................................................................................................
.......................................................................................................
.......................................................................................................
.......................................................................................................
.......................................................................................................
.......................................................................................................
.......................................................................................................
.......................................................................................................
.......................................................................................................
.......................................................................................................
.......................................................................................................

Was this dream...   a recurring dream?   a lucid dream?   a nightmare?
　　　　　　　　　　 ☐ Yes  ☐ No      ☐ Yes  ☐ No    ☐ Yes  ☐ No

## What were the key themes or issues in the dream?

......................................................................................................................

......................................................................................................................

......................................................................................................................

## What were your prominent emotions and feelings?

| | | | | |
|---|---|---|---|---|
| ☐ Happiness | ☐ Surprise | ☐ Indifference | ☐ Fear | ☐ Disapproval |
| ☐ Love | ☐ Joy | ☐ Sadness | ☐ Panic | ☐ Rejection |
| ☐ Freedom | ☐ Contentment | ☐ Frustration | ☐ Envy | ☐ Anxiety |
| ☐ Compassion | ☐ Pride | ☐ Betrayal | ☐ Jealousy | ☐ Guilt |
| ☐ Arousal | ☐ Confusion | ☐ Anger | ☐ Shame | ☐ Pain |
| Other? | ☐ ............ | | ☐ ............ | |
| | ☐ ............ | | ☐ ............ | |

## Could this dream relate to a recent situation/event/person/problem in your life?

......................................................................................................................

......................................................................................................................

......................................................................................................................

## What is your interpretation of the dream?

......................................................................................................................

......................................................................................................................

......................................................................................................................

......................................................................................................................

......................................................................................................................

......................................................................................................................

## In what way(s) does this dream affect you?
### Does it provide clarity into something or suggest a specific course of action?

......................................................................................................................

......................................................................................................................

......................................................................................................................

Dream title: _____  Date: _____

## Dream description

...........................................................................................................................
...........................................................................................................................
...........................................................................................................................
...........................................................................................................................
...........................................................................................................................
...........................................................................................................................
...........................................................................................................................
...........................................................................................................................
...........................................................................................................................
...........................................................................................................................
...........................................................................................................................
...........................................................................................................................
...........................................................................................................................
...........................................................................................................................
...........................................................................................................................
...........................................................................................................................
...........................................................................................................................
...........................................................................................................................
...........................................................................................................................
...........................................................................................................................
...........................................................................................................................
...........................................................................................................................
...........................................................................................................................
...........................................................................................................................
...........................................................................................................................
...........................................................................................................................
...........................................................................................................................
...........................................................................................................................
...........................................................................................................................
...........................................................................................................................

| Was this dream... | a recurring dream? | a lucid dream? | a nightmare? |
|---|---|---|---|
| | ☐ Yes ☐ No | ☐ Yes ☐ No | ☐ Yes ☐ No |

## What were the key themes or issues in the dream?

..............................................................................................................

..............................................................................................................

..............................................................................................................

## What were your prominent emotions and feelings?

| | | | | |
|---|---|---|---|---|
| ☐ Happiness | ☐ Surprise | ☐ Indifference | ☐ Fear | ☐ Disapproval |
| ☐ Love | ☐ Joy | ☐ Sadness | ☐ Panic | ☐ Rejection |
| ☐ Freedom | ☐ Contentment | ☐ Frustration | ☐ Envy | ☐ Anxiety |
| ☐ Compassion | ☐ Pride | ☐ Betrayal | ☐ Jealousy | ☐ Guilt |
| ☐ Arousal | ☐ Confusion | ☐ Anger | ☐ Shame | ☐ Pain |
| Other? | ☐ ................... | | ☐ ................... | |
| | ☐ ................... | | ☐ ................... | |

## Could this dream relate to a recent situation/event/person/problem in your life?

..............................................................................................................

..............................................................................................................

..............................................................................................................

## What is your interpretation of the dream?

..............................................................................................................

..............................................................................................................

..............................................................................................................

..............................................................................................................

..............................................................................................................

..............................................................................................................

..............................................................................................................

## In what way(s) does this dream affect you?
## Does it provide clarity into something or suggest a specific course of action?

..............................................................................................................

..............................................................................................................

..............................................................................................................

Dream title: _____ Date: _____

## Dream description

....................................................................................
....................................................................................
....................................................................................
....................................................................................
....................................................................................
....................................................................................
....................................................................................
....................................................................................
....................................................................................
....................................................................................
....................................................................................
....................................................................................
....................................................................................
....................................................................................
....................................................................................
....................................................................................
....................................................................................
....................................................................................
....................................................................................
....................................................................................
....................................................................................
....................................................................................
....................................................................................
....................................................................................
....................................................................................
....................................................................................
....................................................................................
....................................................................................
....................................................................................
....................................................................................
....................................................................................
....................................................................................

Was this dream...     a recurring dream?     a lucid dream?     a nightmare?
                      ☐ Yes  ☐ No           ☐ Yes  ☐ No        ☐ Yes  ☐ No

## What were the key themes or issues in the dream?

...................................................................................................................

...................................................................................................................

...................................................................................................................

## What were your prominent emotions and feelings?

| | | | | |
|---|---|---|---|---|
| ☐ Happiness | ☐ Surprise | ☐ Indifference | ☐ Fear | ☐ Disapproval |
| ☐ Love | ☐ Joy | ☐ Sadness | ☐ Panic | ☐ Rejection |
| ☐ Freedom | ☐ Contentment | ☐ Frustration | ☐ Envy | ☐ Anxiety |
| ☐ Compassion | ☐ Pride | ☐ Betrayal | ☐ Jealousy | ☐ Guilt |
| ☐ Arousal | ☐ Confusion | ☐ Anger | ☐ Shame | ☐ Pain |
| Other? | ☐ ................ | | ☐ ................ | |
| | ☐ ................ | | ☐ ................ | |

## Could this dream relate to a recent situation/event/person/problem in your life?

...................................................................................................................

...................................................................................................................

...................................................................................................................

## What is your interpretation of the dream?

...................................................................................................................

...................................................................................................................

...................................................................................................................

...................................................................................................................

...................................................................................................................

...................................................................................................................

## In what way(s) does this dream affect you?
## Does it provide clarity into something or suggest a specific course of action?

...................................................................................................................

...................................................................................................................

...................................................................................................................

Dream title: _____          Date: _____

## Dream description

..................................................................................................
..................................................................................................
..................................................................................................
..................................................................................................
..................................................................................................
..................................................................................................
..................................................................................................
..................................................................................................
..................................................................................................
..................................................................................................
..................................................................................................
..................................................................................................
..................................................................................................
..................................................................................................
..................................................................................................
..................................................................................................
..................................................................................................
..................................................................................................
..................................................................................................
..................................................................................................
..................................................................................................
..................................................................................................
..................................................................................................
..................................................................................................
..................................................................................................
..................................................................................................
..................................................................................................
..................................................................................................
..................................................................................................
..................................................................................................

Was this dream...    a recurring dream?    a lucid dream?    a nightmare?
☐ Yes  ☐ No    ☐ Yes  ☐ No    ☐ Yes  ☐ No

## What were the key themes or issues in the dream?

...................................................................................................

...................................................................................................

...................................................................................................

## What were your prominent emotions and feelings?

| | | | | |
|---|---|---|---|---|
| ☐ Happiness | ☐ Surprise | ☐ Indifference | ☐ Fear | ☐ Disapproval |
| ☐ Love | ☐ Joy | ☐ Sadness | ☐ Panic | ☐ Rejection |
| ☐ Freedom | ☐ Contentment | ☐ Frustration | ☐ Envy | ☐ Anxiety |
| ☐ Compassion | ☐ Pride | ☐ Betrayal | ☐ Jealousy | ☐ Guilt |
| ☐ Arousal | ☐ Confusion | ☐ Anger | ☐ Shame | ☐ Pain |
| Other? | ☐ .................... | | ☐ .................... | |
| | ☐ .................... | | ☐ .................... | |

## Could this dream relate to a recent situation/event/person/problem in your life?

...................................................................................................

...................................................................................................

...................................................................................................

## What is your interpretation of the dream?

...................................................................................................

...................................................................................................

...................................................................................................

...................................................................................................

...................................................................................................

...................................................................................................

## In what way(s) does this dream affect you?
## Does it provide clarity into something or suggest a specific course of action?

...................................................................................................

...................................................................................................

...................................................................................................

Dream title:                                                    Date:

## Dream description

.................................................................................................
.................................................................................................
.................................................................................................
.................................................................................................
.................................................................................................
.................................................................................................
.................................................................................................
.................................................................................................
.................................................................................................
.................................................................................................
.................................................................................................
.................................................................................................
.................................................................................................
.................................................................................................
.................................................................................................
.................................................................................................
.................................................................................................
.................................................................................................
.................................................................................................
.................................................................................................
.................................................................................................
.................................................................................................
.................................................................................................
.................................................................................................
.................................................................................................
.................................................................................................
.................................................................................................
.................................................................................................
.................................................................................................
.................................................................................................

Was this dream...

| | a recurring dream? | a lucid dream? | a nightmare? |
|---|---|---|---|
| | ☐ Yes  ☐ No | ☐ Yes  ☐ No | ☐ Yes  ☐ No |

## What were the key themes or issues in the dream?

.............................................................................................................

.............................................................................................................

.............................................................................................................

## What were your prominent emotions and feelings?

| | | | | |
|---|---|---|---|---|
| ☐ Happiness | ☐ Surprise | ☐ Indifference | ☐ Fear | ☐ Disapproval |
| ☐ Love | ☐ Joy | ☐ Sadness | ☐ Panic | ☐ Rejection |
| ☐ Freedom | ☐ Contentment | ☐ Frustration | ☐ Envy | ☐ Anxiety |
| ☐ Compassion | ☐ Pride | ☐ Betrayal | ☐ Jealousy | ☐ Guilt |
| ☐ Arousal | ☐ Confusion | ☐ Anger | ☐ Shame | ☐ Pain |

Other?

☐ ...........................................  ☐ ...........................................

☐ ...........................................  ☐ ...........................................

## Could this dream relate to a recent situation/event/person/problem in your life?

.............................................................................................................

.............................................................................................................

.............................................................................................................

## What is your interpretation of the dream?

.............................................................................................................

.............................................................................................................

.............................................................................................................

.............................................................................................................

.............................................................................................................

.............................................................................................................

.............................................................................................................

## In what way(s) does this dream affect you?
## Does it provide clarity into something or suggest a specific course of action?

.............................................................................................................

.............................................................................................................

.............................................................................................................

Dream title: _____     Date: _____

## Dream description

........................................................................................................
........................................................................................................
........................................................................................................
........................................................................................................
........................................................................................................
........................................................................................................
........................................................................................................
........................................................................................................
........................................................................................................
........................................................................................................
........................................................................................................
........................................................................................................
........................................................................................................
........................................................................................................
........................................................................................................
........................................................................................................
........................................................................................................
........................................................................................................
........................................................................................................
........................................................................................................
........................................................................................................
........................................................................................................
........................................................................................................
........................................................................................................
........................................................................................................
........................................................................................................
........................................................................................................
........................................................................................................

Was this dream...

| a recurring dream? | a lucid dream? | a nightmare? |
|---|---|---|
| ☐ Yes ☐ No | ☐ Yes ☐ No | ☐ Yes ☐ No |

## What were the key themes or issues in the dream?

..........................................................................................................................
..........................................................................................................................
..........................................................................................................................

## What were your prominent emotions and feelings?

| ☐ Happiness | ☐ Surprise | ☐ Indifference | ☐ Fear | ☐ Disapproval |
|---|---|---|---|---|
| ☐ Love | ☐ Joy | ☐ Sadness | ☐ Panic | ☐ Rejection |
| ☐ Freedom | ☐ Contentment | ☐ Frustration | ☐ Envy | ☐ Anxiety |
| ☐ Compassion | ☐ Pride | ☐ Betrayal | ☐ Jealousy | ☐ Guilt |
| ☐ Arousal | ☐ Confusion | ☐ Anger | ☐ Shame | ☐ Pain |

Other?

☐ ..................................... ☐ .....................................
☐ ..................................... ☐ .....................................

## Could this dream relate to a recent situation/event/person/problem in your life?

..........................................................................................................................
..........................................................................................................................
..........................................................................................................................

## What is your interpretation of the dream?

..........................................................................................................................
..........................................................................................................................
..........................................................................................................................
..........................................................................................................................
..........................................................................................................................
..........................................................................................................................

## In what way(s) does this dream affect you?
## Does it provide clarity into something or suggest a specific course of action?

..........................................................................................................................
..........................................................................................................................
..........................................................................................................................

Dream title:                                                    Date:

## Dream description

.......................................................................................................
.......................................................................................................
.......................................................................................................
.......................................................................................................
.......................................................................................................
.......................................................................................................
.......................................................................................................
.......................................................................................................
.......................................................................................................
.......................................................................................................
.......................................................................................................
.......................................................................................................
.......................................................................................................
.......................................................................................................
.......................................................................................................
.......................................................................................................
.......................................................................................................
.......................................................................................................
.......................................................................................................
.......................................................................................................
.......................................................................................................
.......................................................................................................
.......................................................................................................
.......................................................................................................
.......................................................................................................
.......................................................................................................
.......................................................................................................
.......................................................................................................
.......................................................................................................
.......................................................................................................
.......................................................................................................
.......................................................................................................

Was this dream...     a recurring dream?    a lucid dream?    a nightmare?

☐ Yes ☐ No    ☐ Yes ☐ No    ☐ Yes ☐ No

## What were the key themes or issues in the dream?

.................................................................................................

.................................................................................................

.................................................................................................

## What were your prominent emotions and feelings?

| | | | | |
|---|---|---|---|---|
| ☐ Happiness | ☐ Surprise | ☐ Indifference | ☐ Fear | ☐ Disapproval |
| ☐ Love | ☐ Joy | ☐ Sadness | ☐ Panic | ☐ Rejection |
| ☐ Freedom | ☐ Contentment | ☐ Frustration | ☐ Envy | ☐ Anxiety |
| ☐ Compassion | ☐ Pride | ☐ Betrayal | ☐ Jealousy | ☐ Guilt |
| ☐ Arousal | ☐ Confusion | ☐ Anger | ☐ Shame | ☐ Pain |
| Other? | ☐ ............... | | ☐ ............... | |
| | ☐ ............... | | ☐ ............... | |

## Could this dream relate to a recent situation/event/person/problem in your life?

.................................................................................................

.................................................................................................

.................................................................................................

## What is your interpretation of the dream?

.................................................................................................

.................................................................................................

.................................................................................................

.................................................................................................

.................................................................................................

.................................................................................................

## In what way(s) does this dream affect you?
## Does it provide clarity into something or suggest a specific course of action?

.................................................................................................

.................................................................................................

.................................................................................................

Dream title: _____ Date: _____

## Dream description

........................................................................................
........................................................................................
........................................................................................
........................................................................................
........................................................................................
........................................................................................
........................................................................................
........................................................................................
........................................................................................
........................................................................................
........................................................................................
........................................................................................
........................................................................................
........................................................................................
........................................................................................
........................................................................................
........................................................................................
........................................................................................
........................................................................................
........................................................................................
........................................................................................
........................................................................................
........................................................................................
........................................................................................
........................................................................................
........................................................................................
........................................................................................
........................................................................................
........................................................................................
........................................................................................
........................................................................................
........................................................................................

Was this dream...    a recurring dream?    a lucid dream?    a nightmare?
☐ Yes  ☐ No    ☐ Yes  ☐ No    ☐ Yes  ☐ No

## What were the key themes or issues in the dream?

..................................................................................................................
..................................................................................................................
..................................................................................................................

## What were your prominent emotions and feelings?

| | | | | |
|---|---|---|---|---|
| ☐ Happiness | ☐ Surprise | ☐ Indifference | ☐ Fear | ☐ Disapproval |
| ☐ Love | ☐ Joy | ☐ Sadness | ☐ Panic | ☐ Rejection |
| ☐ Freedom | ☐ Contentment | ☐ Frustration | ☐ Envy | ☐ Anxiety |
| ☐ Compassion | ☐ Pride | ☐ Betrayal | ☐ Jealousy | ☐ Guilt |
| ☐ Arousal | ☐ Confusion | ☐ Anger | ☐ Shame | ☐ Pain |

Other?
☐ ..........................    ☐ ..........................
☐ ..........................    ☐ ..........................

## Could this dream relate to a recent situation/event/person/problem in your life?

..................................................................................................................
..................................................................................................................
..................................................................................................................

## What is your interpretation of the dream?

..................................................................................................................
..................................................................................................................
..................................................................................................................
..................................................................................................................
..................................................................................................................
..................................................................................................................

## In what way(s) does this dream affect you?
## Does it provide clarity into something or suggest a specific course of action?

..................................................................................................................
..................................................................................................................
..................................................................................................................

Dream title:                                                    Date:

## Dream description

......................................................................................................................................
......................................................................................................................................
......................................................................................................................................
......................................................................................................................................
......................................................................................................................................
......................................................................................................................................
......................................................................................................................................
......................................................................................................................................
......................................................................................................................................
......................................................................................................................................
......................................................................................................................................
......................................................................................................................................
......................................................................................................................................
......................................................................................................................................
......................................................................................................................................
......................................................................................................................................
......................................................................................................................................
......................................................................................................................................
......................................................................................................................................
......................................................................................................................................
......................................................................................................................................
......................................................................................................................................
......................................................................................................................................
......................................................................................................................................
......................................................................................................................................
......................................................................................................................................
......................................................................................................................................
......................................................................................................................................
......................................................................................................................................
......................................................................................................................................
......................................................................................................................................
......................................................................................................................................

Was this dream...    a recurring dream?    a lucid dream?    a nightmare?
☐ Yes  ☐ No          ☐ Yes  ☐ No         ☐ Yes  ☐ No

## What were the key themes or issues in the dream?

.................................................................................................
.................................................................................................
.................................................................................................

## What were your prominent emotions and feelings?

| | | | | |
|---|---|---|---|---|
| ☐ Happiness | ☐ Surprise | ☐ Indifference | ☐ Fear | ☐ Disapproval |
| ☐ Love | ☐ Joy | ☐ Sadness | ☐ Panic | ☐ Rejection |
| ☐ Freedom | ☐ Contentment | ☐ Frustration | ☐ Envy | ☐ Anxiety |
| ☐ Compassion | ☐ Pride | ☐ Betrayal | ☐ Jealousy | ☐ Guilt |
| ☐ Arousal | ☐ Confusion | ☐ Anger | ☐ Shame | ☐ Pain |

Other?    ☐ .........................    ☐ .........................
          ☐ .........................    ☐ .........................

## Could this dream relate to a recent situation/event/person/problem in your life?

.................................................................................................
.................................................................................................
.................................................................................................

## What is your interpretation of the dream?

.................................................................................................
.................................................................................................
.................................................................................................
.................................................................................................
.................................................................................................
.................................................................................................

## In what way(s) does this dream affect you?
## Does it provide clarity into something or suggest a specific course of action?

.................................................................................................
.................................................................................................
.................................................................................................

Dream title: _____                    Date: _____

## Dream description

........................................................................................................................................

........................................................................................................................................

........................................................................................................................................

........................................................................................................................................

........................................................................................................................................

........................................................................................................................................

........................................................................................................................................

........................................................................................................................................

........................................................................................................................................

........................................................................................................................................

........................................................................................................................................

........................................................................................................................................

........................................................................................................................................

........................................................................................................................................

........................................................................................................................................

........................................................................................................................................

........................................................................................................................................

........................................................................................................................................

........................................................................................................................................

........................................................................................................................................

........................................................................................................................................

........................................................................................................................................

........................................................................................................................................

........................................................................................................................................

........................................................................................................................................

........................................................................................................................................

........................................................................................................................................

........................................................................................................................................

Was this dream...        a recurring dream?       a lucid dream?        a nightmare?
                         ☐ Yes  ☐ No              ☐ Yes  ☐ No          ☐ Yes  ☐ No

## What were the key themes or issues in the dream?

..................................................................................................................
..................................................................................................................
..................................................................................................................

## What were your prominent emotions and feelings?

| | | | | |
|---|---|---|---|---|
| ☐ Happiness | ☐ Surprise | ☐ Indifference | ☐ Fear | ☐ Disapproval |
| ☐ Love | ☐ Joy | ☐ Sadness | ☐ Panic | ☐ Rejection |
| ☐ Freedom | ☐ Contentment | ☐ Frustration | ☐ Envy | ☐ Anxiety |
| ☐ Compassion | ☐ Pride | ☐ Betrayal | ☐ Jealousy | ☐ Guilt |
| ☐ Arousal | ☐ Confusion | ☐ Anger | ☐ Shame | ☐ Pain |
| Other? | ☐ ............... | | ☐ ............... | |
| | ☐ ............... | | ☐ ............... | |

## Could this dream relate to a recent situation/event/person/problem in your life?

..................................................................................................................
..................................................................................................................
..................................................................................................................

## What is your interpretation of the dream?

..................................................................................................................
..................................................................................................................
..................................................................................................................
..................................................................................................................
..................................................................................................................
..................................................................................................................

## In what way(s) does this dream affect you?
## Does it provide clarity into something or suggest a specific course of action?

..................................................................................................................
..................................................................................................................
..................................................................................................................

Dream title: _____          Date: _____

## Dream description

........................................................................................
........................................................................................
........................................................................................
........................................................................................
........................................................................................
........................................................................................
........................................................................................
........................................................................................
........................................................................................
........................................................................................
........................................................................................
........................................................................................
........................................................................................
........................................................................................
........................................................................................
........................................................................................
........................................................................................
........................................................................................
........................................................................................
........................................................................................
........................................................................................
........................................................................................
........................................................................................
........................................................................................
........................................................................................
........................................................................................
........................................................................................
........................................................................................
........................................................................................
........................................................................................
........................................................................................
........................................................................................
........................................................................................

Was this dream...    a recurring dream?    a lucid dream?    a nightmare?
☐ Yes  ☐ No    ☐ Yes  ☐ No    ☐ Yes  ☐ No

## What were the key themes or issues in the dream?

................................................................................................................

................................................................................................................

................................................................................................................

## What were your prominent emotions and feelings?

| | | | | |
|---|---|---|---|---|
| ☐ Happiness | ☐ Surprise | ☐ Indifference | ☐ Fear | ☐ Disapproval |
| ☐ Love | ☐ Joy | ☐ Sadness | ☐ Panic | ☐ Rejection |
| ☐ Freedom | ☐ Contentment | ☐ Frustration | ☐ Envy | ☐ Anxiety |
| ☐ Compassion | ☐ Pride | ☐ Betrayal | ☐ Jealousy | ☐ Guilt |
| ☐ Arousal | ☐ Confusion | ☐ Anger | ☐ Shame | ☐ Pain |
| Other? | ☐ .............. | | ☐ .............. | |
| | ☐ .............. | | ☐ .............. | |

## Could this dream relate to a recent situation/event/person/problem in your life?

................................................................................................................

................................................................................................................

................................................................................................................

## What is your interpretation of the dream?

................................................................................................................

................................................................................................................

................................................................................................................

................................................................................................................

................................................................................................................

................................................................................................................

## In what way(s) does this dream affect you?
## Does it provide clarity into something or suggest a specific course of action?

................................................................................................................

................................................................................................................

................................................................................................................

Dream title:                                              Date:

## Dream description

........................................................................................................................
........................................................................................................................
........................................................................................................................
........................................................................................................................
........................................................................................................................
........................................................................................................................
........................................................................................................................
........................................................................................................................
........................................................................................................................
........................................................................................................................
........................................................................................................................
........................................................................................................................
........................................................................................................................
........................................................................................................................
........................................................................................................................
........................................................................................................................
........................................................................................................................
........................................................................................................................
........................................................................................................................
........................................................................................................................
........................................................................................................................
........................................................................................................................
........................................................................................................................
........................................................................................................................
........................................................................................................................
........................................................................................................................
........................................................................................................................
........................................................................................................................
........................................................................................................................
........................................................................................................................
........................................................................................................................
........................................................................................................................

Was this dream...  a recurring dream?  a lucid dream?  a nightmare?

☐ Yes  ☐ No    ☐ Yes  ☐ No    ☐ Yes  ☐ No

## What were the key themes or issues in the dream?

.................................................................................................

.................................................................................................

.................................................................................................

## What were your prominent emotions and feelings?

| | | | | |
|---|---|---|---|---|
| ☐ Happiness | ☐ Surprise | ☐ Indifference | ☐ Fear | ☐ Disapproval |
| ☐ Love | ☐ Joy | ☐ Sadness | ☐ Panic | ☐ Rejection |
| ☐ Freedom | ☐ Contentment | ☐ Frustration | ☐ Envy | ☐ Anxiety |
| ☐ Compassion | ☐ Pride | ☐ Betrayal | ☐ Jealousy | ☐ Guilt |
| ☐ Arousal | ☐ Confusion | ☐ Anger | ☐ Shame | ☐ Pain |
| Other? | ☐ | | ☐ | |
| | ☐ | | ☐ | |

## Could this dream relate to a recent situation/event/person/problem in your life?

.................................................................................................

.................................................................................................

.................................................................................................

## What is your interpretation of the dream?

.................................................................................................

.................................................................................................

.................................................................................................

.................................................................................................

.................................................................................................

.................................................................................................

.................................................................................................

## In what way(s) does this dream affect you?
## Does it provide clarity into something or suggest a specific course of action?

.................................................................................................

.................................................................................................

.................................................................................................

Dream title:                                    Date:

## Dream description

........................................................................................
........................................................................................
........................................................................................
........................................................................................
........................................................................................
........................................................................................
........................................................................................
........................................................................................
........................................................................................
........................................................................................
........................................................................................
........................................................................................
........................................................................................
........................................................................................
........................................................................................
........................................................................................
........................................................................................
........................................................................................
........................................................................................
........................................................................................
........................................................................................
........................................................................................
........................................................................................
........................................................................................
........................................................................................
........................................................................................
........................................................................................
........................................................................................
........................................................................................
........................................................................................
........................................................................................
........................................................................................
........................................................................................

| Was this dream... | a recurring dream? | a lucid dream? | a nightmare? |
|---|---|---|---|
| | ☐ Yes  ☐ No | ☐ Yes  ☐ No | ☐ Yes  ☐ No |

## What were the key themes or issues in the dream?

..........................................................................................................................................

..........................................................................................................................................

..........................................................................................................................................

## What were your prominent emotions and feelings?

| | | | | |
|---|---|---|---|---|
| ☐ Happiness | ☐ Surprise | ☐ Indifference | ☐ Fear | ☐ Disapproval |
| ☐ Love | ☐ Joy | ☐ Sadness | ☐ Panic | ☐ Rejection |
| ☐ Freedom | ☐ Contentment | ☐ Frustration | ☐ Envy | ☐ Anxiety |
| ☐ Compassion | ☐ Pride | ☐ Betrayal | ☐ Jealousy | ☐ Guilt |
| ☐ Arousal | ☐ Confusion | ☐ Anger | ☐ Shame | ☐ Pain |

Other?

☐ ...................................      ☐ ...................................

☐ ...................................      ☐ ...................................

## Could this dream relate to a recent situation/event/person/problem in your life?

..........................................................................................................................................

..........................................................................................................................................

..........................................................................................................................................

## What is your interpretation of the dream?

..........................................................................................................................................

..........................................................................................................................................

..........................................................................................................................................

..........................................................................................................................................

..........................................................................................................................................

..........................................................................................................................................

..........................................................................................................................................

## In what way(s) does this dream affect you?
## Does it provide clarity into something or suggest a specific course of action?

..........................................................................................................................................

..........................................................................................................................................

..........................................................................................................................................

Dream title:                                             Date:

Dream description

| Was this dream... | a recurring dream?<br>☐ Yes ☐ No | a lucid dream?<br>☐ Yes ☐ No | a nightmare?<br>☐ Yes ☐ No |
|---|---|---|---|

## What were the key themes or issues in the dream?

..............................................................................................................

..............................................................................................................

..............................................................................................................

## What were your prominent emotions and feelings?

| ☐ Happiness | ☐ Surprise | ☐ Indifference | ☐ Fear | ☐ Disapproval |
|---|---|---|---|---|
| ☐ Love | ☐ Joy | ☐ Sadness | ☐ Panic | ☐ Rejection |
| ☐ Freedom | ☐ Contentment | ☐ Frustration | ☐ Envy | ☐ Anxiety |
| ☐ Compassion | ☐ Pride | ☐ Betrayal | ☐ Jealousy | ☐ Guilt |
| ☐ Arousal | ☐ Confusion | ☐ Anger | ☐ Shame | ☐ Pain |
| Other? | ☐ ................. | | ☐ ................. | |
| | ☐ ................. | | ☐ ................. | |

## Could this dream relate to a recent situation/event/person/problem in your life?

..............................................................................................................

..............................................................................................................

..............................................................................................................

## What is your interpretation of the dream?

..............................................................................................................

..............................................................................................................

..............................................................................................................

..............................................................................................................

..............................................................................................................

..............................................................................................................

..............................................................................................................

## In what way(s) does this dream affect you?
## Does it provide clarity into something or suggest a specific course of action?

..............................................................................................................

..............................................................................................................

..............................................................................................................

Dream title: _____          Date: _____

## Dream description

...........................................................................................................................

...........................................................................................................................

...........................................................................................................................

...........................................................................................................................

...........................................................................................................................

...........................................................................................................................

...........................................................................................................................

...........................................................................................................................

...........................................................................................................................

...........................................................................................................................

...........................................................................................................................

...........................................................................................................................

...........................................................................................................................

...........................................................................................................................

...........................................................................................................................

...........................................................................................................................

...........................................................................................................................

...........................................................................................................................

...........................................................................................................................

...........................................................................................................................

...........................................................................................................................

...........................................................................................................................

...........................................................................................................................

...........................................................................................................................

...........................................................................................................................

...........................................................................................................................

...........................................................................................................................

...........................................................................................................................

...........................................................................................................................

...........................................................................................................................

...........................................................................................................................

...........................................................................................................................

...........................................................................................................................

...........................................................................................................................

Was this dream...  a recurring dream?  a lucid dream?  a nightmare?
☐ Yes  ☐ No  ☐ Yes  ☐ No  ☐ Yes  ☐ No

## What were the key themes or issues in the dream?

.............................................................................................................

.............................................................................................................

.............................................................................................................

## What were your prominent emotions and feelings?

| | | | | |
|---|---|---|---|---|
| ☐ Happiness | ☐ Surprise | ☐ Indifference | ☐ Fear | ☐ Disapproval |
| ☐ Love | ☐ Joy | ☐ Sadness | ☐ Panic | ☐ Rejection |
| ☐ Freedom | ☐ Contentment | ☐ Frustration | ☐ Envy | ☐ Anxiety |
| ☐ Compassion | ☐ Pride | ☐ Betrayal | ☐ Jealousy | ☐ Guilt |
| ☐ Arousal | ☐ Confusion | ☐ Anger | ☐ Shame | ☐ Pain |

Other?  ☐ ..........................................  ☐ ..........................................
☐ ..........................................  ☐ ..........................................

## Could this dream relate to a recent situation/event/person/problem in your life?

.............................................................................................................

.............................................................................................................

.............................................................................................................

## What is your interpretation of the dream?

.............................................................................................................

.............................................................................................................

.............................................................................................................

.............................................................................................................

.............................................................................................................

.............................................................................................................

.............................................................................................................

## In what way(s) does this dream affect you?
## Does it provide clarity into something or suggest a specific course of action?

.............................................................................................................

.............................................................................................................

.............................................................................................................

Dream title:                                                    Date:

## Dream description

......................................................................................................................
......................................................................................................................
......................................................................................................................
......................................................................................................................
......................................................................................................................
......................................................................................................................
......................................................................................................................
......................................................................................................................
......................................................................................................................
......................................................................................................................
......................................................................................................................
......................................................................................................................
......................................................................................................................
......................................................................................................................
......................................................................................................................
......................................................................................................................
......................................................................................................................
......................................................................................................................
......................................................................................................................
......................................................................................................................
......................................................................................................................
......................................................................................................................
......................................................................................................................
......................................................................................................................
......................................................................................................................
......................................................................................................................
......................................................................................................................
......................................................................................................................
......................................................................................................................
......................................................................................................................
......................................................................................................................
......................................................................................................................
......................................................................................................................

Was this dream...    a recurring dream?    a lucid dream?    a nightmare?
☐ Yes  ☐ No      ☐ Yes  ☐ No      ☐ Yes  ☐ No

## What were the key themes or issues in the dream?

.................................................................................................................................

.................................................................................................................................

.................................................................................................................................

## What were your prominent emotions and feelings?

| | | | | |
|---|---|---|---|---|
| ☐ Happiness | ☐ Surprise | ☐ Indifference | ☐ Fear | ☐ Disapproval |
| ☐ Love | ☐ Joy | ☐ Sadness | ☐ Panic | ☐ Rejection |
| ☐ Freedom | ☐ Contentment | ☐ Frustration | ☐ Envy | ☐ Anxiety |
| ☐ Compassion | ☐ Pride | ☐ Betrayal | ☐ Jealousy | ☐ Guilt |
| ☐ Arousal | ☐ Confusion | ☐ Anger | ☐ Shame | ☐ Pain |

Other?    ☐ ................................   ☐ ................................

☐ ................................   ☐ ................................

## Could this dream relate to a recent situation/event/person/problem in your life?

.................................................................................................................................

.................................................................................................................................

.................................................................................................................................

## What is your interpretation of the dream?

.................................................................................................................................

.................................................................................................................................

.................................................................................................................................

.................................................................................................................................

.................................................................................................................................

.................................................................................................................................

.................................................................................................................................

## In what way(s) does this dream affect you?
## Does it provide clarity into something or suggest a specific course of action?

.................................................................................................................................

.................................................................................................................................

.................................................................................................................................

Dream title: _____ Date: _____

Dream description
_____

....................................................................

....................................................................

....................................................................

....................................................................

....................................................................

....................................................................

....................................................................

....................................................................

....................................................................

....................................................................

....................................................................

....................................................................

....................................................................

....................................................................

....................................................................

....................................................................

....................................................................

....................................................................

....................................................................

....................................................................

....................................................................

....................................................................

....................................................................

....................................................................

....................................................................

....................................................................

....................................................................

....................................................................

....................................................................

....................................................................

....................................................................

....................................................................

....................................................................

....................................................................

....................................................................

Was this dream...      a recurring dream?      a lucid dream?      a nightmare?
                       ☐ Yes  ☐ No            ☐ Yes  ☐ No         ☐ Yes  ☐ No

## What were the key themes or issues in the dream?

................................................................

................................................................

................................................................

## What were your prominent emotions and feelings?

| | | | | |
|---|---|---|---|---|
| ☐ Happiness | ☐ Surprise | ☐ Indifference | ☐ Fear | ☐ Disapproval |
| ☐ Love | ☐ Joy | ☐ Sadness | ☐ Panic | ☐ Rejection |
| ☐ Freedom | ☐ Contentment | ☐ Frustration | ☐ Envy | ☐ Anxiety |
| ☐ Compassion | ☐ Pride | ☐ Betrayal | ☐ Jealousy | ☐ Guilt |
| ☐ Arousal | ☐ Confusion | ☐ Anger | ☐ Shame | ☐ Pain |
| Other? | ☐ | | ☐ | |
| | ☐ | | ☐ | |

## Could this dream relate to a recent situation/event/person/problem in your life?

................................................................

................................................................

................................................................

## What is your interpretation of the dream?

................................................................

................................................................

................................................................

................................................................

................................................................

................................................................

## In what way(s) does this dream affect you?
## Does it provide clarity into something or suggest a specific course of action?

................................................................

................................................................

................................................................

Dream title: _____ Date: _____

## Dream description

........................................................................................
........................................................................................
........................................................................................
........................................................................................
........................................................................................
........................................................................................
........................................................................................
........................................................................................
........................................................................................
........................................................................................
........................................................................................
........................................................................................
........................................................................................
........................................................................................
........................................................................................
........................................................................................
........................................................................................
........................................................................................
........................................................................................
........................................................................................
........................................................................................
........................................................................................
........................................................................................
........................................................................................
........................................................................................
........................................................................................
........................................................................................
........................................................................................
........................................................................................
........................................................................................
........................................................................................
........................................................................................
........................................................................................

Was this dream...

| | a recurring dream? | a lucid dream? | a nightmare? |
|---|---|---|---|
| | ☐ Yes  ☐ No | ☐ Yes  ☐ No | ☐ Yes  ☐ No |

## What were the key themes or issues in the dream?

...................................................................................................................

...................................................................................................................

...................................................................................................................

## What were your prominent emotions and feelings?

| | | | | |
|---|---|---|---|---|
| ☐ Happiness | ☐ Surprise | ☐ Indifference | ☐ Fear | ☐ Disapproval |
| ☐ Love | ☐ Joy | ☐ Sadness | ☐ Panic | ☐ Rejection |
| ☐ Freedom | ☐ Contentment | ☐ Frustration | ☐ Envy | ☐ Anxiety |
| ☐ Compassion | ☐ Pride | ☐ Betrayal | ☐ Jealousy | ☐ Guilt |
| ☐ Arousal | ☐ Confusion | ☐ Anger | ☐ Shame | ☐ Pain |
| Other? | ☐ ................... | | ☐ ................... | |
| | ☐ ................... | | ☐ ................... | |

## Could this dream relate to a recent situation/event/person/problem in your life?

...................................................................................................................

...................................................................................................................

...................................................................................................................

## What is your interpretation of the dream?

...................................................................................................................

...................................................................................................................

...................................................................................................................

...................................................................................................................

...................................................................................................................

...................................................................................................................

## In what way(s) does this dream affect you?
## Does it provide clarity into something or suggest a specific course of action?

...................................................................................................................

...................................................................................................................

...................................................................................................................

Dream title:                                                    Date:

Dream description

Was this dream...     a recurring dream?     a lucid dream?     a nightmare?
                      ☐ Yes  ☐ No           ☐ Yes  ☐ No        ☐ Yes  ☐ No

## What were the key themes or issues in the dream?

..................................................................................................................

..................................................................................................................

..................................................................................................................

## What were your prominent emotions and feelings?

☐ Happiness    ☐ Surprise      ☐ Indifference   ☐ Fear        ☐ Disapproval

☐ Love         ☐ Joy           ☐ Sadness        ☐ Panic       ☐ Rejection

☐ Freedom      ☐ Contentment   ☐ Frustration    ☐ Envy        ☐ Anxiety

☐ Compassion   ☐ Pride         ☐ Betrayal       ☐ Jealousy    ☐ Guilt

☐ Arousal      ☐ Confusion     ☐ Anger          ☐ Shame       ☐ Pain

Other?         ☐                                 ☐
                 ..............................     ..............................
               ☐                                 ☐
                 ..............................     ..............................

## Could this dream relate to a recent situation/event/person/problem in your life?

..................................................................................................................

..................................................................................................................

..................................................................................................................

## What is your interpretation of the dream?

..................................................................................................................

..................................................................................................................

..................................................................................................................

..................................................................................................................

..................................................................................................................

..................................................................................................................

## In what way(s) does this dream affect you?
## Does it provide clarity into something or suggest a specific course of action?

..................................................................................................................

..................................................................................................................

..................................................................................................................

Dream title: _____     Date: _____

## Dream description

.....................................................................................................
.....................................................................................................
.....................................................................................................
.....................................................................................................
.....................................................................................................
.....................................................................................................
.....................................................................................................
.....................................................................................................
.....................................................................................................
.....................................................................................................
.....................................................................................................
.....................................................................................................
.....................................................................................................
.....................................................................................................
.....................................................................................................
.....................................................................................................
.....................................................................................................
.....................................................................................................
.....................................................................................................
.....................................................................................................
.....................................................................................................
.....................................................................................................
.....................................................................................................
.....................................................................................................
.....................................................................................................
.....................................................................................................
.....................................................................................................
.....................................................................................................
.....................................................................................................
.....................................................................................................
.....................................................................................................
.....................................................................................................
.....................................................................................................

Was this dream... a recurring dream? a lucid dream? a nightmare?
☐ Yes ☐ No ☐ Yes ☐ No ☐ Yes ☐ No

## What were the key themes or issues in the dream?

..............................................................................................................................

..............................................................................................................................

..............................................................................................................................

## What were your prominent emotions and feelings?

| | | | | |
|---|---|---|---|---|
| ☐ Happiness | ☐ Surprise | ☐ Indifference | ☐ Fear | ☐ Disapproval |
| ☐ Love | ☐ Joy | ☐ Sadness | ☐ Panic | ☐ Rejection |
| ☐ Freedom | ☐ Contentment | ☐ Frustration | ☐ Envy | ☐ Anxiety |
| ☐ Compassion | ☐ Pride | ☐ Betrayal | ☐ Jealousy | ☐ Guilt |
| ☐ Arousal | ☐ Confusion | ☐ Anger | ☐ Shame | ☐ Pain |

Other?
☐ ........................................ ☐ ........................................
☐ ........................................ ☐ ........................................

## Could this dream relate to a recent situation/event/person/problem in your life?

..............................................................................................................................

..............................................................................................................................

..............................................................................................................................

## What is your interpretation of the dream?

..............................................................................................................................

..............................................................................................................................

..............................................................................................................................

..............................................................................................................................

..............................................................................................................................

..............................................................................................................................

..............................................................................................................................

## In what way(s) does this dream affect you?
## Does it provide clarity into something or suggest a specific course of action?

..............................................................................................................................

..............................................................................................................................

..............................................................................................................................

Dream title:                                                    Date:

## Dream description

..............................................................................................
..............................................................................................
..............................................................................................
..............................................................................................
..............................................................................................
..............................................................................................
..............................................................................................
..............................................................................................
..............................................................................................
..............................................................................................
..............................................................................................
..............................................................................................
..............................................................................................
..............................................................................................
..............................................................................................
..............................................................................................
..............................................................................................
..............................................................................................
..............................................................................................
..............................................................................................
..............................................................................................
..............................................................................................
..............................................................................................
..............................................................................................
..............................................................................................
..............................................................................................
..............................................................................................
..............................................................................................
..............................................................................................
..............................................................................................
..............................................................................................
..............................................................................................

Was this dream...   a recurring dream?     a lucid dream?          a nightmare?
                    ☐ Yes   ☐ No          ☐ Yes   ☐ No            ☐ Yes   ☐ No

## What were the key themes or issues in the dream?

...........................................................................................................................

...........................................................................................................................

...........................................................................................................................

## What were your prominent emotions and feelings?

| | | | | |
|---|---|---|---|---|
| ☐ Happiness | ☐ Surprise | ☐ Indifference | ☐ Fear | ☐ Disapproval |
| ☐ Love | ☐ Joy | ☐ Sadness | ☐ Panic | ☐ Rejection |
| ☐ Freedom | ☐ Contentment | ☐ Frustration | ☐ Envy | ☐ Anxiety |
| ☐ Compassion | ☐ Pride | ☐ Betrayal | ☐ Jealousy | ☐ Guilt |
| ☐ Arousal | ☐ Confusion | ☐ Anger | ☐ Shame | ☐ Pain |

Other?      ☐ ....................................   ☐ ....................................
            ☐ ....................................   ☐ ....................................

## Could this dream relate to a recent situation/event/person/problem in your life?

...........................................................................................................................

...........................................................................................................................

...........................................................................................................................

## What is your interpretation of the dream?

...........................................................................................................................

...........................................................................................................................

...........................................................................................................................

...........................................................................................................................

...........................................................................................................................

...........................................................................................................................

## In what way(s) does this dream affect you?
## Does it provide clarity into something or suggest a specific course of action?

...........................................................................................................................

...........................................................................................................................

...........................................................................................................................

Dream title: _____                    Date: _____

Dream description

································································································
································································································
································································································
································································································
································································································
································································································
································································································
································································································
································································································
································································································
································································································
································································································
································································································
································································································
································································································
································································································
································································································
································································································
································································································
································································································
································································································
································································································
································································································
································································································
································································································
································································································
································································································
································································································
································································································
································································································
································································································
································································································
································································································

Was this dream...    a recurring dream?    a lucid dream?    a nightmare?

☐ Yes ☐ No    ☐ Yes ☐ No    ☐ Yes ☐ No

## What were the key themes or issues in the dream?

..................................................................................................................

..................................................................................................................

..................................................................................................................

## What were your prominent emotions and feelings?

| | | | | |
|---|---|---|---|---|
| ☐ Happiness | ☐ Surprise | ☐ Indifference | ☐ Fear | ☐ Disapproval |
| ☐ Love | ☐ Joy | ☐ Sadness | ☐ Panic | ☐ Rejection |
| ☐ Freedom | ☐ Contentment | ☐ Frustration | ☐ Envy | ☐ Anxiety |
| ☐ Compassion | ☐ Pride | ☐ Betrayal | ☐ Jealousy | ☐ Guilt |
| ☐ Arousal | ☐ Confusion | ☐ Anger | ☐ Shame | ☐ Pain |
| Other? | ☐ .......... | | ☐ .......... | |
| | ☐ .......... | | ☐ .......... | |

## Could this dream relate to a recent situation/event/person/problem in your life?

..................................................................................................................

..................................................................................................................

..................................................................................................................

## What is your interpretation of the dream?

..................................................................................................................

..................................................................................................................

..................................................................................................................

..................................................................................................................

..................................................................................................................

..................................................................................................................

..................................................................................................................

## In what way(s) does this dream affect you?
## Does it provide clarity into something or suggest a specific course of action?

..................................................................................................................

..................................................................................................................

..................................................................................................................

Dream title:                                              Date:

## Dream description

..............................................................................................................................

..............................................................................................................................

..............................................................................................................................

..............................................................................................................................

..............................................................................................................................

..............................................................................................................................

..............................................................................................................................

..............................................................................................................................

..............................................................................................................................

..............................................................................................................................

..............................................................................................................................

..............................................................................................................................

..............................................................................................................................

..............................................................................................................................

..............................................................................................................................

..............................................................................................................................

..............................................................................................................................

..............................................................................................................................

..............................................................................................................................

..............................................................................................................................

..............................................................................................................................

..............................................................................................................................

..............................................................................................................................

..............................................................................................................................

..............................................................................................................................

..............................................................................................................................

..............................................................................................................................

..............................................................................................................................

..............................................................................................................................

..............................................................................................................................

..............................................................................................................................

..............................................................................................................................

..............................................................................................................................

Was this dream...	a recurring dream?	a lucid dream?	a nightmare?
☐ Yes ☐ No	☐ Yes ☐ No	☐ Yes ☐ No

## What were the key themes or issues in the dream?

...................................................................................................................

...................................................................................................................

...................................................................................................................

## What were your prominent emotions and feelings?

| | | | | |
|---|---|---|---|---|
| ☐ Happiness | ☐ Surprise | ☐ Indifference | ☐ Fear | ☐ Disapproval |
| ☐ Love | ☐ Joy | ☐ Sadness | ☐ Panic | ☐ Rejection |
| ☐ Freedom | ☐ Contentment | ☐ Frustration | ☐ Envy | ☐ Anxiety |
| ☐ Compassion | ☐ Pride | ☐ Betrayal | ☐ Jealousy | ☐ Guilt |
| ☐ Arousal | ☐ Confusion | ☐ Anger | ☐ Shame | ☐ Pain |
| Other? | ☐ | | ☐ | |
| | ☐ | | ☐ | |

## Could this dream relate to a recent situation/event/person/problem in your life?

...................................................................................................................

...................................................................................................................

...................................................................................................................

## What is your interpretation of the dream?

...................................................................................................................

...................................................................................................................

...................................................................................................................

...................................................................................................................

...................................................................................................................

...................................................................................................................

## In what way(s) does this dream affect you?
## Does it provide clarity into something or suggest a specific course of action?

...................................................................................................................

...................................................................................................................

...................................................................................................................

Dream title:                                          Date:

Dream description

Was this dream...    a recurring dream?    a lucid dream?    a nightmare?
☐ Yes  ☐ No    ☐ Yes  ☐ No    ☐ Yes  ☐ No

## What were the key themes or issues in the dream?

.................................................................................

.................................................................................

.................................................................................

## What were your prominent emotions and feelings?

| | | | | |
|---|---|---|---|---|
| ☐ Happiness | ☐ Surprise | ☐ Indifference | ☐ Fear | ☐ Disapproval |
| ☐ Love | ☐ Joy | ☐ Sadness | ☐ Panic | ☐ Rejection |
| ☐ Freedom | ☐ Contentment | ☐ Frustration | ☐ Envy | ☐ Anxiety |
| ☐ Compassion | ☐ Pride | ☐ Betrayal | ☐ Jealousy | ☐ Guilt |
| ☐ Arousal | ☐ Confusion | ☐ Anger | ☐ Shame | ☐ Pain |

Other?    ☐ .......................    ☐ .......................

☐ .......................    ☐ .......................

## Could this dream relate to a recent situation/event/person/problem in your life?

.................................................................................

.................................................................................

.................................................................................

## What is your interpretation of the dream?

.................................................................................

.................................................................................

.................................................................................

.................................................................................

.................................................................................

.................................................................................

.................................................................................

## In what way(s) does this dream affect you?
## Does it provide clarity into something or suggest a specific course of action?

.................................................................................

.................................................................................

.................................................................................

Dream title: _____ Date: _____

## Dream description

........................................................................................
........................................................................................
........................................................................................
........................................................................................
........................................................................................
........................................................................................
........................................................................................
........................................................................................
........................................................................................
........................................................................................
........................................................................................
........................................................................................
........................................................................................
........................................................................................
........................................................................................
........................................................................................
........................................................................................
........................................................................................
........................................................................................
........................................................................................
........................................................................................
........................................................................................
........................................................................................
........................................................................................
........................................................................................
........................................................................................
........................................................................................
........................................................................................
........................................................................................
........................................................................................
........................................................................................
........................................................................................
........................................................................................
........................................................................................
........................................................................................
........................................................................................

Was this dream...    a recurring dream?        a lucid dream?        a nightmare?
                     ☐ Yes  ☐ No              ☐ Yes  ☐ No          ☐ Yes  ☐ No

## What were the key themes or issues in the dream?

..............................................................................................
..............................................................................................
..............................................................................................

## What were your prominent emotions and feelings?

| | | | | |
|---|---|---|---|---|
| ☐ Happiness | ☐ Surprise | ☐ Indifference | ☐ Fear | ☐ Disapproval |
| ☐ Love | ☐ Joy | ☐ Sadness | ☐ Panic | ☐ Rejection |
| ☐ Freedom | ☐ Contentment | ☐ Frustration | ☐ Envy | ☐ Anxiety |
| ☐ Compassion | ☐ Pride | ☐ Betrayal | ☐ Jealousy | ☐ Guilt |
| ☐ Arousal | ☐ Confusion | ☐ Anger | ☐ Shame | ☐ Pain |

Other?    ☐ ...........................    ☐ ...........................
          ☐ ...........................    ☐ ...........................

## Could this dream relate to a recent situation/event/person/problem in your life?

..............................................................................................
..............................................................................................
..............................................................................................

## What is your interpretation of the dream?

..............................................................................................
..............................................................................................
..............................................................................................
..............................................................................................
..............................................................................................
..............................................................................................
..............................................................................................

## In what way(s) does this dream affect you?
## Does it provide clarity into something or suggest a specific course of action?

..............................................................................................
..............................................................................................
..............................................................................................

Dream title:                                          Date:

## Dream description

..........................................................................................................................................
..........................................................................................................................................
..........................................................................................................................................
..........................................................................................................................................
..........................................................................................................................................
..........................................................................................................................................
..........................................................................................................................................
..........................................................................................................................................
..........................................................................................................................................
..........................................................................................................................................
..........................................................................................................................................
..........................................................................................................................................
..........................................................................................................................................
..........................................................................................................................................
..........................................................................................................................................
..........................................................................................................................................
..........................................................................................................................................
..........................................................................................................................................
..........................................................................................................................................
..........................................................................................................................................
..........................................................................................................................................
..........................................................................................................................................
..........................................................................................................................................
..........................................................................................................................................
..........................................................................................................................................
..........................................................................................................................................
..........................................................................................................................................
..........................................................................................................................................
..........................................................................................................................................
..........................................................................................................................................
..........................................................................................................................................
..........................................................................................................................................
..........................................................................................................................................

Was this dream...    a recurring dream?    a lucid dream?    a nightmare?

☐ Yes ☐ No    ☐ Yes ☐ No    ☐ Yes ☐ No

## What were the key themes or issues in the dream?

...................................................................................................................

...................................................................................................................

...................................................................................................................

## What were your prominent emotions and feelings?

| | | | | |
|---|---|---|---|---|
| ☐ Happiness | ☐ Surprise | ☐ Indifference | ☐ Fear | ☐ Disapproval |
| ☐ Love | ☐ Joy | ☐ Sadness | ☐ Panic | ☐ Rejection |
| ☐ Freedom | ☐ Contentment | ☐ Frustration | ☐ Envy | ☐ Anxiety |
| ☐ Compassion | ☐ Pride | ☐ Betrayal | ☐ Jealousy | ☐ Guilt |
| ☐ Arousal | ☐ Confusion | ☐ Anger | ☐ Shame | ☐ Pain |
| Other? | ☐ ................... | | ☐ ................... | |
| | ☐ ................... | | ☐ ................... | |

## Could this dream relate to a recent situation/event/person/problem in your life?

...................................................................................................................

...................................................................................................................

...................................................................................................................

## What is your interpretation of the dream?

...................................................................................................................

...................................................................................................................

...................................................................................................................

...................................................................................................................

...................................................................................................................

...................................................................................................................

...................................................................................................................

## In what way(s) does this dream affect you?
## Does it provide clarity into something or suggest a specific course of action?

...................................................................................................................

...................................................................................................................

...................................................................................................................

Dream title:                                                      Date:

Dream description

........................................................................................
........................................................................................
........................................................................................
........................................................................................
........................................................................................
........................................................................................
........................................................................................
........................................................................................
........................................................................................
........................................................................................
........................................................................................
........................................................................................
........................................................................................
........................................................................................
........................................................................................
........................................................................................
........................................................................................
........................................................................................
........................................................................................
........................................................................................
........................................................................................
........................................................................................
........................................................................................
........................................................................................
........................................................................................
........................................................................................
........................................................................................
........................................................................................
........................................................................................
........................................................................................
........................................................................................
........................................................................................
........................................................................................
........................................................................................

Was this dream...    a recurring dream?    a lucid dream?    a nightmare?
                     ☐ Yes  ☐ No          ☐ Yes  ☐ No       ☐ Yes  ☐ No

## What were the key themes or issues in the dream?

...................................................................................................................

...................................................................................................................

...................................................................................................................

## What were your prominent emotions and feelings?

| | | | | |
|---|---|---|---|---|
| ☐ Happiness | ☐ Surprise | ☐ Indifference | ☐ Fear | ☐ Disapproval |
| ☐ Love | ☐ Joy | ☐ Sadness | ☐ Panic | ☐ Rejection |
| ☐ Freedom | ☐ Contentment | ☐ Frustration | ☐ Envy | ☐ Anxiety |
| ☐ Compassion | ☐ Pride | ☐ Betrayal | ☐ Jealousy | ☐ Guilt |
| ☐ Arousal | ☐ Confusion | ☐ Anger | ☐ Shame | ☐ Pain |

Other?    ☐ ..................................    ☐ ..................................

          ☐ ..................................    ☐ ..................................

## Could this dream relate to a recent situation/event/person/problem in your life?

...................................................................................................................

...................................................................................................................

...................................................................................................................

## What is your interpretation of the dream?

...................................................................................................................

...................................................................................................................

...................................................................................................................

...................................................................................................................

...................................................................................................................

...................................................................................................................

...................................................................................................................

## In what way(s) does this dream affect you?
## Does it provide clarity into something or suggest a specific course of action?

...................................................................................................................

...................................................................................................................

...................................................................................................................

Dream title: _____                    Date: _____

## Dream description

........................................................................................
........................................................................................
........................................................................................
........................................................................................
........................................................................................
........................................................................................
........................................................................................
........................................................................................
........................................................................................
........................................................................................
........................................................................................
........................................................................................
........................................................................................
........................................................................................
........................................................................................
........................................................................................
........................................................................................
........................................................................................
........................................................................................
........................................................................................
........................................................................................
........................................................................................
........................................................................................
........................................................................................
........................................................................................
........................................................................................
........................................................................................
........................................................................................
........................................................................................
........................................................................................
........................................................................................
........................................................................................
........................................................................................
........................................................................................
........................................................................................
........................................................................................
........................................................................................
........................................................................................
........................................................................................

Was this dream...   a recurring dream?   a lucid dream?   a nightmare?
　　　　　　　　　　　☐ Yes ☐ No   ☐ Yes ☐ No   ☐ Yes ☐ No

## What were the key themes or issues in the dream?

...............................................................................................................................

...............................................................................................................................

...............................................................................................................................

## What were your prominent emotions and feelings?

| ☐ Happiness | ☐ Surprise | ☐ Indifference | ☐ Fear | ☐ Disapproval |
| ☐ Love | ☐ Joy | ☐ Sadness | ☐ Panic | ☐ Rejection |
| ☐ Freedom | ☐ Contentment | ☐ Frustration | ☐ Envy | ☐ Anxiety |
| ☐ Compassion | ☐ Pride | ☐ Betrayal | ☐ Jealousy | ☐ Guilt |
| ☐ Arousal | ☐ Confusion | ☐ Anger | ☐ Shame | ☐ Pain |
| Other? | ☐ | | ☐ | |
| | ☐ | | ☐ | |

## Could this dream relate to a recent situation/event/person/problem in your life?

...............................................................................................................................

...............................................................................................................................

...............................................................................................................................

## What is your interpretation of the dream?

...............................................................................................................................

...............................................................................................................................

...............................................................................................................................

...............................................................................................................................

...............................................................................................................................

...............................................................................................................................

...............................................................................................................................

## In what way(s) does this dream affect you?
## Does it provide clarity into something or suggest a specific course of action?

...............................................................................................................................

...............................................................................................................................

...............................................................................................................................

Dream title: _____    Date: _____

## Dream description

........................................................................................................
........................................................................................................
........................................................................................................
........................................................................................................
........................................................................................................
........................................................................................................
........................................................................................................
........................................................................................................
........................................................................................................
........................................................................................................
........................................................................................................
........................................................................................................
........................................................................................................
........................................................................................................
........................................................................................................
........................................................................................................
........................................................................................................
........................................................................................................
........................................................................................................
........................................................................................................
........................................................................................................
........................................................................................................
........................................................................................................
........................................................................................................
........................................................................................................
........................................................................................................
........................................................................................................
........................................................................................................
........................................................................................................
........................................................................................................
........................................................................................................
........................................................................................................
........................................................................................................

Was this dream...	a recurring dream?	a lucid dream?	a nightmare?
☐ Yes  ☐ No	☐ Yes  ☐ No	☐ Yes  ☐ No

## What were the key themes or issues in the dream?

..................................................................................................

..................................................................................................

..................................................................................................

## What were your prominent emotions and feelings?

| ☐ Happiness | ☐ Surprise | ☐ Indifference | ☐ Fear | ☐ Disapproval |
|---|---|---|---|---|
| ☐ Love | ☐ Joy | ☐ Sadness | ☐ Panic | ☐ Rejection |
| ☐ Freedom | ☐ Contentment | ☐ Frustration | ☐ Envy | ☐ Anxiety |
| ☐ Compassion | ☐ Pride | ☐ Betrayal | ☐ Jealousy | ☐ Guilt |
| ☐ Arousal | ☐ Confusion | ☐ Anger | ☐ Shame | ☐ Pain |

Other?	☐ ...........................................	☐ ...........................................

☐ ...........................................	☐ ...........................................

## Could this dream relate to a recent situation/event/person/problem in your life?

..................................................................................................

..................................................................................................

..................................................................................................

## What is your interpretation of the dream?

..................................................................................................

..................................................................................................

..................................................................................................

..................................................................................................

..................................................................................................

..................................................................................................

..................................................................................................

## In what way(s) does this dream affect you?
## Does it provide clarity into something or suggest a specific course of action?

..................................................................................................

..................................................................................................

..................................................................................................

Dream title:                                    Date:

_____

Dream description
_____

....................................................................................
....................................................................................
....................................................................................
....................................................................................
....................................................................................
....................................................................................
....................................................................................
....................................................................................
....................................................................................
....................................................................................
....................................................................................
....................................................................................
....................................................................................
....................................................................................
....................................................................................
....................................................................................
....................................................................................
....................................................................................
....................................................................................
....................................................................................
....................................................................................
....................................................................................
....................................................................................
....................................................................................
....................................................................................
....................................................................................
....................................................................................
....................................................................................
....................................................................................
....................................................................................
....................................................................................
....................................................................................
....................................................................................
....................................................................................

Was this dream...

| | a recurring dream? | a lucid dream? | a nightmare? |
|---|---|---|---|
| | ☐ Yes  ☐ No | ☐ Yes  ☐ No | ☐ Yes  ☐ No |

## What were the key themes or issues in the dream?

......................................................................................................................

......................................................................................................................

......................................................................................................................

## What were your prominent emotions and feelings?

| | | | | |
|---|---|---|---|---|
| ☐ Happiness | ☐ Surprise | ☐ Indifference | ☐ Fear | ☐ Disapproval |
| ☐ Love | ☐ Joy | ☐ Sadness | ☐ Panic | ☐ Rejection |
| ☐ Freedom | ☐ Contentment | ☐ Frustration | ☐ Envy | ☐ Anxiety |
| ☐ Compassion | ☐ Pride | ☐ Betrayal | ☐ Jealousy | ☐ Guilt |
| ☐ Arousal | ☐ Confusion | ☐ Anger | ☐ Shame | ☐ Pain |

Other?        ☐ ...............................  ☐ ...............................

              ☐ ...............................  ☐ ...............................

## Could this dream relate to a recent situation/event/person/problem in your life?

......................................................................................................................

......................................................................................................................

......................................................................................................................

## What is your interpretation of the dream?

......................................................................................................................

......................................................................................................................

......................................................................................................................

......................................................................................................................

......................................................................................................................

......................................................................................................................

......................................................................................................................

## In what way(s) does this dream affect you?
## Does it provide clarity into something or suggest a specific course of action?

......................................................................................................................

......................................................................................................................

......................................................................................................................

Dream title:                                    Date:

## Dream description

........................................................................................................
........................................................................................................
........................................................................................................
........................................................................................................
........................................................................................................
........................................................................................................
........................................................................................................
........................................................................................................
........................................................................................................
........................................................................................................
........................................................................................................
........................................................................................................
........................................................................................................
........................................................................................................
........................................................................................................
........................................................................................................
........................................................................................................
........................................................................................................
........................................................................................................
........................................................................................................
........................................................................................................
........................................................................................................
........................................................................................................
........................................................................................................
........................................................................................................
........................................................................................................
........................................................................................................
........................................................................................................
........................................................................................................
........................................................................................................
........................................................................................................
........................................................................................................
........................................................................................................

Was this dream...

| a recurring dream? | a lucid dream? | a nightmare? |
|---|---|---|
| ☐ Yes ☐ No | ☐ Yes ☐ No | ☐ Yes ☐ No |

## What were the key themes or issues in the dream?

..................................................................................................................

..................................................................................................................

..................................................................................................................

## What were your prominent emotions and feelings?

| | | | | |
|---|---|---|---|---|
| ☐ Happiness | ☐ Surprise | ☐ Indifference | ☐ Fear | ☐ Disapproval |
| ☐ Love | ☐ Joy | ☐ Sadness | ☐ Panic | ☐ Rejection |
| ☐ Freedom | ☐ Contentment | ☐ Frustration | ☐ Envy | ☐ Anxiety |
| ☐ Compassion | ☐ Pride | ☐ Betrayal | ☐ Jealousy | ☐ Guilt |
| ☐ Arousal | ☐ Confusion | ☐ Anger | ☐ Shame | ☐ Pain |
| Other? | ☐ ................................ | | ☐ ................................ | |
| | ☐ ................................ | | ☐ ................................ | |

## Could this dream relate to a recent situation/event/person/problem in your life?

..................................................................................................................

..................................................................................................................

..................................................................................................................

## What is your interpretation of the dream?

..................................................................................................................

..................................................................................................................

..................................................................................................................

..................................................................................................................

..................................................................................................................

..................................................................................................................

..................................................................................................................

## In what way(s) does this dream affect you?
## Does it provide clarity into something or suggest a specific course of action?

..................................................................................................................

..................................................................................................................

..................................................................................................................

Dream title:                                                    Date:

Dream description

........................................................................................................................
........................................................................................................................
........................................................................................................................
........................................................................................................................
........................................................................................................................
........................................................................................................................
........................................................................................................................
........................................................................................................................
........................................................................................................................
........................................................................................................................
........................................................................................................................
........................................................................................................................
........................................................................................................................
........................................................................................................................
........................................................................................................................
........................................................................................................................
........................................................................................................................
........................................................................................................................
........................................................................................................................
........................................................................................................................
........................................................................................................................
........................................................................................................................
........................................................................................................................
........................................................................................................................
........................................................................................................................
........................................................................................................................
........................................................................................................................
........................................................................................................................
........................................................................................................................
........................................................................................................................
........................................................................................................................
........................................................................................................................

Was this dream...

| a recurring dream? | a lucid dream? | a nightmare? |
|---|---|---|
| ☐ Yes  ☐ No | ☐ Yes  ☐ No | ☐ Yes  ☐ No |

## What were the key themes or issues in the dream?

..................................................................................................

..................................................................................................

..................................................................................................

## What were your prominent emotions and feelings?

| | | | | |
|---|---|---|---|---|
| ☐ Happiness | ☐ Surprise | ☐ Indifference | ☐ Fear | ☐ Disapproval |
| ☐ Love | ☐ Joy | ☐ Sadness | ☐ Panic | ☐ Rejection |
| ☐ Freedom | ☐ Contentment | ☐ Frustration | ☐ Envy | ☐ Anxiety |
| ☐ Compassion | ☐ Pride | ☐ Betrayal | ☐ Jealousy | ☐ Guilt |
| ☐ Arousal | ☐ Confusion | ☐ Anger | ☐ Shame | ☐ Pain |

Other?

☐ .......................................... ☐ ..........................................

☐ .......................................... ☐ ..........................................

## Could this dream relate to a recent situation/event/person/problem in your life?

..................................................................................................

..................................................................................................

..................................................................................................

## What is your interpretation of the dream?

..................................................................................................

..................................................................................................

..................................................................................................

..................................................................................................

..................................................................................................

..................................................................................................

..................................................................................................

## In what way(s) does this dream affect you?
## Does it provide clarity into something or suggest a specific course of action?

..................................................................................................

..................................................................................................

..................................................................................................

Dream title: _____     Date: _____

## Dream description

...........................................................................................................................................................
...........................................................................................................................................................
...........................................................................................................................................................
...........................................................................................................................................................
...........................................................................................................................................................
...........................................................................................................................................................
...........................................................................................................................................................
...........................................................................................................................................................
...........................................................................................................................................................
...........................................................................................................................................................
...........................................................................................................................................................
...........................................................................................................................................................
...........................................................................................................................................................
...........................................................................................................................................................
...........................................................................................................................................................
...........................................................................................................................................................
...........................................................................................................................................................
...........................................................................................................................................................
...........................................................................................................................................................
...........................................................................................................................................................
...........................................................................................................................................................
...........................................................................................................................................................
...........................................................................................................................................................
...........................................................................................................................................................
...........................................................................................................................................................
...........................................................................................................................................................
...........................................................................................................................................................
...........................................................................................................................................................
...........................................................................................................................................................
...........................................................................................................................................................
...........................................................................................................................................................
...........................................................................................................................................................
...........................................................................................................................................................

Was this dream...    a recurring dream?    a lucid dream?    a nightmare?
                ☐ Yes   ☐ No     ☐ Yes   ☐ No     ☐ Yes   ☐ No

## What were the key themes or issues in the dream?

..............................................................................................................................

..............................................................................................................................

..............................................................................................................................

## What were your prominent emotions and feelings?

| ☐ Happiness | ☐ Surprise | ☐ Indifference | ☐ Fear | ☐ Disapproval |
|---|---|---|---|---|
| ☐ Love | ☐ Joy | ☐ Sadness | ☐ Panic | ☐ Rejection |
| ☐ Freedom | ☐ Contentment | ☐ Frustration | ☐ Envy | ☐ Anxiety |
| ☐ Compassion | ☐ Pride | ☐ Betrayal | ☐ Jealousy | ☐ Guilt |
| ☐ Arousal | ☐ Confusion | ☐ Anger | ☐ Shame | ☐ Pain |

Other?    ☐ ............................    ☐ ............................

         ☐ ............................    ☐ ............................

## Could this dream relate to a recent situation/event/person/problem in your life?

..............................................................................................................................

..............................................................................................................................

..............................................................................................................................

## What is your interpretation of the dream?

..............................................................................................................................

..............................................................................................................................

..............................................................................................................................

..............................................................................................................................

..............................................................................................................................

..............................................................................................................................

..............................................................................................................................

## In what way(s) does this dream affect you?
## Does it provide clarity into something or suggest a specific course of action?

..............................................................................................................................

..............................................................................................................................

..............................................................................................................................

Dream title: _____ Date: _____

## Dream description

.......................................................................................
.......................................................................................
.......................................................................................
.......................................................................................
.......................................................................................
.......................................................................................
.......................................................................................
.......................................................................................
.......................................................................................
.......................................................................................
.......................................................................................
.......................................................................................
.......................................................................................
.......................................................................................
.......................................................................................
.......................................................................................
.......................................................................................
.......................................................................................
.......................................................................................
.......................................................................................
.......................................................................................
.......................................................................................
.......................................................................................
.......................................................................................
.......................................................................................
.......................................................................................
.......................................................................................
.......................................................................................
.......................................................................................
.......................................................................................
.......................................................................................

Was this dream...    a recurring dream?    a lucid dream?    a nightmare?
☐ Yes  ☐ No    ☐ Yes  ☐ No    ☐ Yes  ☐ No

## What were the key themes or issues in the dream?

..............................................................................................................................

..............................................................................................................................

..............................................................................................................................

## What were your prominent emotions and feelings?

| | | | | |
|---|---|---|---|---|
| ☐ Happiness | ☐ Surprise | ☐ Indifference | ☐ Fear | ☐ Disapproval |
| ☐ Love | ☐ Joy | ☐ Sadness | ☐ Panic | ☐ Rejection |
| ☐ Freedom | ☐ Contentment | ☐ Frustration | ☐ Envy | ☐ Anxiety |
| ☐ Compassion | ☐ Pride | ☐ Betrayal | ☐ Jealousy | ☐ Guilt |
| ☐ Arousal | ☐ Confusion | ☐ Anger | ☐ Shame | ☐ Pain |

Other?    ☐ ......................................    ☐ ......................................

☐ ......................................    ☐ ......................................

## Could this dream relate to a recent situation/event/person/problem in your life?

..............................................................................................................................

..............................................................................................................................

..............................................................................................................................

## What is your interpretation of the dream?

..............................................................................................................................

..............................................................................................................................

..............................................................................................................................

..............................................................................................................................

..............................................................................................................................

..............................................................................................................................

..............................................................................................................................

## In what way(s) does this dream affect you?
## Does it provide clarity into something or suggest a specific course of action?

..............................................................................................................................

..............................................................................................................................

..............................................................................................................................

Dream title:                                              Date:

Dream description

..................................................................................................................................
..................................................................................................................................
..................................................................................................................................
..................................................................................................................................
..................................................................................................................................
..................................................................................................................................
..................................................................................................................................
..................................................................................................................................
..................................................................................................................................
..................................................................................................................................
..................................................................................................................................
..................................................................................................................................
..................................................................................................................................
..................................................................................................................................
..................................................................................................................................
..................................................................................................................................
..................................................................................................................................
..................................................................................................................................
..................................................................................................................................
..................................................................................................................................
..................................................................................................................................
..................................................................................................................................
..................................................................................................................................
..................................................................................................................................
..................................................................................................................................
..................................................................................................................................
..................................................................................................................................
..................................................................................................................................
..................................................................................................................................
..................................................................................................................................
..................................................................................................................................

Was this dream...  a recurring dream?  a lucid dream?  a nightmare?
☐ Yes  ☐ No      ☐ Yes  ☐ No      ☐ Yes  ☐ No

## What were the key themes or issues in the dream?

.............................................................................................................

.............................................................................................................

.............................................................................................................

## What were your prominent emotions and feelings?

| ☐ Happiness | ☐ Surprise | ☐ Indifference | ☐ Fear | ☐ Disapproval |
| ☐ Love | ☐ Joy | ☐ Sadness | ☐ Panic | ☐ Rejection |
| ☐ Freedom | ☐ Contentment | ☐ Frustration | ☐ Envy | ☐ Anxiety |
| ☐ Compassion | ☐ Pride | ☐ Betrayal | ☐ Jealousy | ☐ Guilt |
| ☐ Arousal | ☐ Confusion | ☐ Anger | ☐ Shame | ☐ Pain |

Other?
☐ ......................................  ☐ ......................................
☐ ......................................  ☐ ......................................

## Could this dream relate to a recent situation/event/person/problem in your life?

.............................................................................................................

.............................................................................................................

.............................................................................................................

## What is your interpretation of the dream?

.............................................................................................................

.............................................................................................................

.............................................................................................................

.............................................................................................................

.............................................................................................................

.............................................................................................................

.............................................................................................................

## In what way(s) does this dream affect you?
## Does it provide clarity into something or suggest a specific course of action?

.............................................................................................................

.............................................................................................................

.............................................................................................................

Dream title: _____ Date: _____

## Dream description

...............................................................................................................
...............................................................................................................
...............................................................................................................
...............................................................................................................
...............................................................................................................
...............................................................................................................
...............................................................................................................
...............................................................................................................
...............................................................................................................
...............................................................................................................
...............................................................................................................
...............................................................................................................
...............................................................................................................
...............................................................................................................
...............................................................................................................
...............................................................................................................
...............................................................................................................
...............................................................................................................
...............................................................................................................
...............................................................................................................
...............................................................................................................
...............................................................................................................
...............................................................................................................
...............................................................................................................
...............................................................................................................
...............................................................................................................
...............................................................................................................
...............................................................................................................
...............................................................................................................
...............................................................................................................
...............................................................................................................
...............................................................................................................
...............................................................................................................

Was this dream...  a recurring dream?  a lucid dream?  a nightmare?
☐ Yes  ☐ No  ☐ Yes  ☐ No  ☐ Yes  ☐ No

## What were the key themes or issues in the dream?

.......................................................................................................................................

.......................................................................................................................................

.......................................................................................................................................

## What were your prominent emotions and feelings?

| | | | | |
|---|---|---|---|---|
| ☐ Happiness | ☐ Surprise | ☐ Indifference | ☐ Fear | ☐ Disapproval |
| ☐ Love | ☐ Joy | ☐ Sadness | ☐ Panic | ☐ Rejection |
| ☐ Freedom | ☐ Contentment | ☐ Frustration | ☐ Envy | ☐ Anxiety |
| ☐ Compassion | ☐ Pride | ☐ Betrayal | ☐ Jealousy | ☐ Guilt |
| ☐ Arousal | ☐ Confusion | ☐ Anger | ☐ Shame | ☐ Pain |
| Other? | ☐ ...................... | | ☐ ...................... | |
| | ☐ ...................... | | ☐ ...................... | |

## Could this dream relate to a recent situation/event/person/problem in your life?

.......................................................................................................................................

.......................................................................................................................................

.......................................................................................................................................

## What is your interpretation of the dream?

.......................................................................................................................................

.......................................................................................................................................

.......................................................................................................................................

.......................................................................................................................................

.......................................................................................................................................

.......................................................................................................................................

.......................................................................................................................................

## In what way(s) does this dream affect you?
## Does it provide clarity into something or suggest a specific course of action?

.......................................................................................................................................

.......................................................................................................................................

.......................................................................................................................................

**Dream title:**                                    **Date:**

### Dream description

Was this dream...          a recurring dream?       a lucid dream?       a nightmare?
                           ☐ Yes   ☐ No            ☐ Yes   ☐ No        ☐ Yes   ☐ No

## What were the key themes or issues in the dream?

..................................................................................................................
..................................................................................................................
..................................................................................................................

## What were your prominent emotions and feelings?

☐ Happiness      ☐ Surprise        ☐ Indifference      ☐ Fear          ☐ Disapproval
☐ Love           ☐ Joy             ☐ Sadness           ☐ Panic         ☐ Rejection
☐ Freedom        ☐ Contentment     ☐ Frustration       ☐ Envy          ☐ Anxiety
☐ Compassion     ☐ Pride           ☐ Betrayal          ☐ Jealousy      ☐ Guilt
☐ Arousal        ☐ Confusion       ☐ Anger             ☐ Shame         ☐ Pain
Other?           ☐                                     ☐
                 ☐ .............................        ☐ .............................

## Could this dream relate to a recent situation/event/person/problem in your life?

..................................................................................................................
..................................................................................................................
..................................................................................................................

## What is your interpretation of the dream?

..................................................................................................................
..................................................................................................................
..................................................................................................................
..................................................................................................................
..................................................................................................................
..................................................................................................................

## In what way(s) does this dream affect you?
## Does it provide clarity into something or suggest a specific course of action?

..................................................................................................................
..................................................................................................................
..................................................................................................................

Dream title: _____  Date: _____

## Dream description

.......................................................................................................................
.......................................................................................................................
.......................................................................................................................
.......................................................................................................................
.......................................................................................................................
.......................................................................................................................
.......................................................................................................................
.......................................................................................................................
.......................................................................................................................
.......................................................................................................................
.......................................................................................................................
.......................................................................................................................
.......................................................................................................................
.......................................................................................................................
.......................................................................................................................
.......................................................................................................................
.......................................................................................................................
.......................................................................................................................
.......................................................................................................................
.......................................................................................................................
.......................................................................................................................
.......................................................................................................................
.......................................................................................................................
.......................................................................................................................
.......................................................................................................................
.......................................................................................................................
.......................................................................................................................
.......................................................................................................................
.......................................................................................................................
.......................................................................................................................

Was this dream...        a recurring dream?        a lucid dream?        a nightmare?
                         ☐ Yes  ☐ No              ☐ Yes  ☐ No          ☐ Yes  ☐ No

## What were the key themes or issues in the dream?

.............................................................................................................................
.............................................................................................................................
.............................................................................................................................

## What were your prominent emotions and feelings?

| ☐ Happiness | ☐ Surprise | ☐ Indifference | ☐ Fear | ☐ Disapproval |
| ☐ Love | ☐ Joy | ☐ Sadness | ☐ Panic | ☐ Rejection |
| ☐ Freedom | ☐ Contentment | ☐ Frustration | ☐ Envy | ☐ Anxiety |
| ☐ Compassion | ☐ Pride | ☐ Betrayal | ☐ Jealousy | ☐ Guilt |
| ☐ Arousal | ☐ Confusion | ☐ Anger | ☐ Shame | ☐ Pain |

Other?        ☐ ...........................        ☐ ...........................
              ☐ ...........................        ☐ ...........................

## Could this dream relate to a recent situation/event/person/problem in your life?

.............................................................................................................................
.............................................................................................................................
.............................................................................................................................

## What is your interpretation of the dream?

.............................................................................................................................
.............................................................................................................................
.............................................................................................................................
.............................................................................................................................
.............................................................................................................................
.............................................................................................................................
.............................................................................................................................

## In what way(s) does this dream affect you?
## Does it provide clarity into something or suggest a specific course of action?

.............................................................................................................................
.............................................................................................................................
.............................................................................................................................

Dream title: _____ Date: _____

## Dream description

........................................................................................................
........................................................................................................
........................................................................................................
........................................................................................................
........................................................................................................
........................................................................................................
........................................................................................................
........................................................................................................
........................................................................................................
........................................................................................................
........................................................................................................
........................................................................................................
........................................................................................................
........................................................................................................
........................................................................................................
........................................................................................................
........................................................................................................
........................................................................................................
........................................................................................................
........................................................................................................
........................................................................................................
........................................................................................................
........................................................................................................
........................................................................................................
........................................................................................................
........................................................................................................
........................................................................................................
........................................................................................................
........................................................................................................
........................................................................................................
........................................................................................................
........................................................................................................

Was this dream...    a recurring dream?    a lucid dream?    a nightmare?
                                ☐ Yes  ☐ No    ☐ Yes  ☐ No    ☐ Yes  ☐ No

## What were the key themes or issues in the dream?

....................................................................................................................

....................................................................................................................

....................................................................................................................

## What were your prominent emotions and feelings?

| | | | | |
|---|---|---|---|---|
| ☐ Happiness | ☐ Surprise | ☐ Indifference | ☐ Fear | ☐ Disapproval |
| ☐ Love | ☐ Joy | ☐ Sadness | ☐ Panic | ☐ Rejection |
| ☐ Freedom | ☐ Contentment | ☐ Frustration | ☐ Envy | ☐ Anxiety |
| ☐ Compassion | ☐ Pride | ☐ Betrayal | ☐ Jealousy | ☐ Guilt |
| ☐ Arousal | ☐ Confusion | ☐ Anger | ☐ Shame | ☐ Pain |

Other?

☐ ...............................................    ☐ ...............................................

☐ ...............................................    ☐ ...............................................

## Could this dream relate to a recent situation/event/person/problem in your life?

....................................................................................................................

....................................................................................................................

....................................................................................................................

## What is your interpretation of the dream?

....................................................................................................................

....................................................................................................................

....................................................................................................................

....................................................................................................................

....................................................................................................................

....................................................................................................................

....................................................................................................................

## In what way(s) does this dream affect you?
### Does it provide clarity into something or suggest a specific course of action?

....................................................................................................................

....................................................................................................................

....................................................................................................................

Dream title:                            Date:

## Dream description

...........................................................................................................................

...........................................................................................................................

...........................................................................................................................

...........................................................................................................................

...........................................................................................................................

...........................................................................................................................

...........................................................................................................................

...........................................................................................................................

...........................................................................................................................

...........................................................................................................................

...........................................................................................................................

...........................................................................................................................

...........................................................................................................................

...........................................................................................................................

...........................................................................................................................

...........................................................................................................................

...........................................................................................................................

...........................................................................................................................

...........................................................................................................................

...........................................................................................................................

...........................................................................................................................

...........................................................................................................................

...........................................................................................................................

...........................................................................................................................

...........................................................................................................................

...........................................................................................................................

...........................................................................................................................

...........................................................................................................................

...........................................................................................................................

...........................................................................................................................

...........................................................................................................................

...........................................................................................................................

Was this dream...
a recurring dream?
☐ Yes ☐ No

a lucid dream?
☐ Yes ☐ No

a nightmare?
☐ Yes ☐ No

## What were the key themes or issues in the dream?

..............................................................................................................................................

..............................................................................................................................................

..............................................................................................................................................

## What were your prominent emotions and feelings?

☐ Happiness      ☐ Surprise        ☐ Indifference     ☐ Fear         ☐ Disapproval

☐ Love           ☐ Joy             ☐ Sadness          ☐ Panic        ☐ Rejection

☐ Freedom        ☐ Contentment     ☐ Frustration      ☐ Envy         ☐ Anxiety

☐ Compassion     ☐ Pride           ☐ Betrayal         ☐ Jealousy     ☐ Guilt

☐ Arousal        ☐ Confusion       ☐ Anger            ☐ Shame        ☐ Pain

Other?           ☐                                     ☐
                    ........................              ........................
                 ☐                                     ☐
                    ........................              ........................

## Could this dream relate to a recent situation/event/person/problem in your life?

..............................................................................................................................................

..............................................................................................................................................

..............................................................................................................................................

## What is your interpretation of the dream?

..............................................................................................................................................

..............................................................................................................................................

..............................................................................................................................................

..............................................................................................................................................

..............................................................................................................................................

..............................................................................................................................................

..............................................................................................................................................

## In what way(s) does this dream affect you?
## Does it provide clarity into something or suggest a specific course of action?

..............................................................................................................................................

..............................................................................................................................................

..............................................................................................................................................

Dream title: _____      Date: _____

## Dream description

......................................................................................................
......................................................................................................
......................................................................................................
......................................................................................................
......................................................................................................
......................................................................................................
......................................................................................................
......................................................................................................
......................................................................................................
......................................................................................................
......................................................................................................
......................................................................................................
......................................................................................................
......................................................................................................
......................................................................................................
......................................................................................................
......................................................................................................
......................................................................................................
......................................................................................................
......................................................................................................
......................................................................................................
......................................................................................................
......................................................................................................
......................................................................................................
......................................................................................................
......................................................................................................
......................................................................................................
......................................................................................................
......................................................................................................
......................................................................................................
......................................................................................................
......................................................................................................
......................................................................................................

Was this dream...
| a recurring dream? | a lucid dream? | a nightmare? |
|---|---|---|
| ☐ Yes ☐ No | ☐ Yes ☐ No | ☐ Yes ☐ No |

## What were the key themes or issues in the dream?

..................................................................................................................................

..................................................................................................................................

..................................................................................................................................

## What were your prominent emotions and feelings?

| ☐ Happiness | ☐ Surprise | ☐ Indifference | ☐ Fear | ☐ Disapproval |
|---|---|---|---|---|
| ☐ Love | ☐ Joy | ☐ Sadness | ☐ Panic | ☐ Rejection |
| ☐ Freedom | ☐ Contentment | ☐ Frustration | ☐ Envy | ☐ Anxiety |
| ☐ Compassion | ☐ Pride | ☐ Betrayal | ☐ Jealousy | ☐ Guilt |
| ☐ Arousal | ☐ Confusion | ☐ Anger | ☐ Shame | ☐ Pain |

Other?
☐ ..................................  ☐ ..................................
☐ ..................................  ☐ ..................................

## Could this dream relate to a recent situation/event/person/problem in your life?

..................................................................................................................................

..................................................................................................................................

..................................................................................................................................

## What is your interpretation of the dream?

..................................................................................................................................

..................................................................................................................................

..................................................................................................................................

..................................................................................................................................

..................................................................................................................................

..................................................................................................................................

## In what way(s) does this dream affect you?
## Does it provide clarity into something or suggest a specific course of action?

..................................................................................................................................

..................................................................................................................................

..................................................................................................................................

Dream title: _____   Date: _____

## Dream description

......................................................................................................
......................................................................................................
......................................................................................................
......................................................................................................
......................................................................................................
......................................................................................................
......................................................................................................
......................................................................................................
......................................................................................................
......................................................................................................
......................................................................................................
......................................................................................................
......................................................................................................
......................................................................................................
......................................................................................................
......................................................................................................
......................................................................................................
......................................................................................................
......................................................................................................
......................................................................................................
......................................................................................................
......................................................................................................
......................................................................................................
......................................................................................................
......................................................................................................
......................................................................................................
......................................................................................................
......................................................................................................
......................................................................................................
......................................................................................................
......................................................................................................
......................................................................................................
......................................................................................................

Was this dream...  a recurring dream?   a lucid dream?   a nightmare?
☐ Yes  ☐ No   ☐ Yes  ☐ No   ☐ Yes  ☐ No

## What were the key themes or issues in the dream?

......................................................................................................................

......................................................................................................................

......................................................................................................................

## What were your prominent emotions and feelings?

| | | | | |
|---|---|---|---|---|
| ☐ Happiness | ☐ Surprise | ☐ Indifference | ☐ Fear | ☐ Disapproval |
| ☐ Love | ☐ Joy | ☐ Sadness | ☐ Panic | ☐ Rejection |
| ☐ Freedom | ☐ Contentment | ☐ Frustration | ☐ Envy | ☐ Anxiety |
| ☐ Compassion | ☐ Pride | ☐ Betrayal | ☐ Jealousy | ☐ Guilt |
| ☐ Arousal | ☐ Confusion | ☐ Anger | ☐ Shame | ☐ Pain |
| Other? | ☐ .................. | | ☐ .................. | |
| | ☐ .................. | | ☐ .................. | |

## Could this dream relate to a recent situation/event/person/problem in your life?

......................................................................................................................

......................................................................................................................

......................................................................................................................

## What is your interpretation of the dream?

......................................................................................................................

......................................................................................................................

......................................................................................................................

......................................................................................................................

......................................................................................................................

......................................................................................................................

## In what way(s) does this dream affect you?
## Does it provide clarity into something or suggest a specific course of action?

......................................................................................................................

......................................................................................................................

......................................................................................................................

57915271R00071

Made in the USA
San Bernardino, CA
22 November 2017